BOOKS BY A. BARTLETT GIAMATTI

The University and the
Public Interest

A. Bartlett Giamatti

THE UNIVERSITY AND THE PUBLIC INTEREST

Atheneum New York 1981

*All of the contents, with the exception of "The
Private University and the Public Interest" and
"Coda: The Codification of Us All," previously
appeared in the* Yale Alumni Magazine & Journal.
*"The American Teacher" also appeared in the
July 1980 issue of* Harper's Magazine

Library of Congress Cataloging in Publication Data

Giamatti, A. Bartlett.
    The university and the public interest.

    1. Education, Higher—United States—Aims and
objectives.   2.   Education—United States—Aims and
objectives.   I.   Title.
LB2328.2.G5   378'.01'0973   81-66030
ISBN 0-689-11212-2   AACR2

To *J. Richardson Dilworth*

Preface

These various essays contain no new legislative programs for action, no policy initiatives. They were, for the most part, written at different times in the last three years, for different occasions, with one common goal: to explore the nature of our institutions for education and the purposes for which those institutions are intended. The institutions themselves are varied: language is one, private universities another, the federal government yet another, and our public schools. I am concerned with the civic goals of education, by which I mean that set of intellectual processes that are infused with a set of values, values American and humane. If there is a unity to this extended essay, made up of diverse forays, it is a unity that derives from a set of private convictions that education in America is a powerful force for good and is the way to arrive at a forceful public good.

I am concerned throughout with connections, between principles and practicalities, schools and governments, students and teachers, language and power, restraint and release. I am concerned with the way limits must be loved not for the pressures they impose on us but for the liberality toward which they can urge us. There is, therefore, a good deal of dealing in paradox in this collection, and no small amount of what it means to have as a working assumption that we live in a fallen state, whose ambiguities are a joy. The reader who does not share my sense of the need for certain contradictory connections, who does not agree that independence and regulation in all things must go together, will find not ambiguity but confusion here. Thus there will be, for some, self-canceling assertions about the centrality of language and the need for precision in its interpretation and composition, and about not believing everything need be written down or codified. There will be for some too much etymologizing about words or institutions in order to define the new contours that must emerge in institutions or words if America is to be as full of grace as it is materially generous. With the charge that in some ways I see the country, through education, as having a great past before it, I agree, because I do not believe we can afford to fail to remember what our aspirations have been, else our acts will be mean.

The basic assumption running through all these

perspectives is that the educational process, like the country it animates, is an act of the will, fusing access and structure, democratic values and hierarchical modes of governance, convictions about excellence and about equity, into a single, variegated, generous ideal. These essays contain no programmatic initiatives, because the most practical part of the American soul is its capacity to assert and live by principles. Education in this country has been a way of constantly defining that process of pragmatic idealism and has been a central version of what that tradition means. If in thinking about education in its various forms, especially from the standpoint of a private university, I have been educated in the process, and the marks of my education are visible, so be it. The mind in motion, tending to the condition of affirming its unique individual shape while wishing to promote a humane commonwealth, is in many ways my subject.

One last word about the local references in some of these explorations. I refer to Yale because it is the place I know best. I do not presume to think it is the only place wishing to do good while wanting to do well; I do not expect or wish the reader to read Yale every time he sees it written. Nor do I think the issues as defined for private educational institutions do not also reach public colleges and universities. Excellence is everywhere and does not inhere necessarily in locality or size or form of charter or foundation. I am, however, someplace, and while I may hope that what follows will have resonance elsewhere and will raise, if not by any means resolve, concerns widely felt and expressed, I can only speak with confidence about Yale. A certain parochialism results, therefore, from insisting on my local habitation and a name. For this parochialism of reference, I ask the reader's indulgence; should the parochialism emerge as more than one of reference, then I will have denied what I wish to assert, that limit may be the path to a humane liberality, to a freedom of spirit and civic action.

These essays all had their origins in speeches for various occasions, and I have not tried to remove all the marks of their beginnings. They have also been revised as they evolved. "The Private University and the Public Interest" was first given in March 1979 at the Department of Health, Education and Welfare and then to the senior class in 1979, as a baccalaureate address; "The Nature and Purpose of the University" was my inaugural address in October 1978; "The Apocalyptic Style" was the freshman address in September 1980; "Sentimentality," one of two pieces not written recently, was first delivered in Washington, D.C. to alumni, and printed in the Yale Alumni Magazine in January 1976; "On Behalf of the Humanities" was first delivered in 1977 at Yale and then given at the Modern Language Association in December 1978; "Nature Justly Viewed" was the freshman address in September 1979; "Yale and Athletics" was delivered in a longer version to the Association of Yale Alumni in April 1980; "Private Sector, Public Control and the Independent University" was delivered as the baccalaureate address to the senior class in 1980; "Science and the University" was delivered to the Association of Yale Alumni in October 1980; "The American Teacher" began as a Phi Beta Kappa lecture at Yale and after many changes was circulated as the Annual Report of the President, March 1980; "The American School" was delivered to a conference on Excellence in Education in the State House, Hartford, Connecticut in January 1981; "Power, Politics and a Sense of History" was delivered as the baccalaureate address to the senior class in 1981; and "Coda: The Codification of Us All" was delivered to the annual gathering of Alumni of the Yale Law School, October 1980.

To the many colleagues and others who have offered comments and corrections in the course of the composition of these essays, my thanks. I particularly extend my gratitude to Henry W. Broude, José A. Cabranes, Michael Cooke, Stanley E. Flink, Toni S. Giamatti, Abraham S. Goldstein, Donald Kagan, Serge Lang and Georges May. They bear no responsibility for what has emerged. Nadine Shimada and Sherry Dombkowski typed and retyped. Regina Starolis, Kathy Straka and Janet Adami kept it all straight. Harry Ford has been an unfailingly courteous and sensitive editor. This book is dedicated to the senior fellow of the Yale Corporation, a peerless trustee and friend and one who embodies the values this volume espouses.

A. Bartlett Giamatti

New Haven, April, 1981

Contents

xiii

The University and the
Public Interest

The Private University and the Public Interest

I intend neither to petition nor to promulgate. I have no new strategy, no new complaint for an old problem or old balm for new wounds. I am neither an adversary nor an appointee of the government. I am an unanointed, lay advocate of the private university. My institution is one of them—by no means the largest, not at all the richest, certainly not the most humble. I am devoted to it, and to places like it, large and small, ancient and modern. I now pass much of my time pondering the futures of such private educational institutions, and the savage pressures that will shape those futures—the pressures of inflation, of demographic decline, of the atrophied opportunities for younger faculty.

To that Homeric catalogue of pressures (I have named only the flagships) I wish today to add another, and to explore its lineaments. It is really a simple irony, forged of all the pressures. In the next difficult years, those private institutions most dedicated by tradition and mandate to spurring the young to public interest will be forced to become the newest special-interest group. To convince sources of public support to support them, for the greater good, they will have to plead even more for their private concerns. They will be driven to it by the will to survive.

And yet does one really want to see it happen? Does one really want to have places of private higher education sustain civic values and necessary basic research; teach the young, and give them a sense of the past so that they may help make the future; continue, in innumerable ways, to reflect and serve the broad interest of the public, only by behaving essentially in a less and less public-spirited way? And yet if a liberal education, and a liberalized professional education, open for the many in the service of all, is to be fostered, then it will only be if such institutions become better at applying, and applying for, special pressure.

Some will rejoice at the spectacle, for a variety of reasons, but such glee will have much more bile than buoyancy in it. It will be mean-spirited glee, and it will avail nothing. For choice is essential to a free society, and choice is reduced to mere chance when survival becomes a function of the amount of pressure one can apply to government. In a society that believes in pluralism, of institutions as well as values, it will be a significant loss when the private impulse toward the public interest will only be sustained by the constitution of special-interest forces. Any system that asks for and rewards fragmentation cries for its own dissolution.

Private universities would not have it so. They want to be self-reliant, responsive to their traditions, responsible to the larger society. Those strands are, historically, the toughest, most resilient threads in their fabric. And the larger society, while wary of them, has always wanted such institutions to flourish, if for no other reason than it wanted the leadership that came from them, and more recently has come to depend upon the goods that flow from research done in them. The larger society has always wanted access to private institutions and it has access to the best of them. Their quality has become part of the national hope. America wishes to think of such private institutions as crucial, though it threatens, through its government, to treat them as if they were public instrumentalities. We should all clearly understand that nothing could be less in the public interest.

The problem is that despite what private universities desire and aside from what the nation requires, such places will have to depend increasingly for student loan and basic research aid upon government. That is why such places will be forced to become more adept at pressuring for their principles. And as they do, what will become clear is not that they have gotten their hands dirty, or wrists slapped, or that they have entered the "system." What will be clearer and clearer to those on all sides who care is how little government understands the nature of private educational institutions.

Of course, the fault for that is not really government's. Private colleges and universities have never adequately educated government, or any number of other segments of society, in the nature of educational institutions, whether public or private, while it is the nature of government to assume that all institutions in a society ought to look like governments. In America, government is accustomed to dealing with itself, with industrial facilities, profit-making corporations, commercial enterprises, big labor, armies. Educational institutions are like none of these. They are built differently, for a different set of purposes, with different histories. They cannot write off losses; they cannot pass all costs along to the consumers; they do not have tables of organization that initiates in such mysteries would recognize as legitimate. They cannot readily shift workers from one part of the plant to another. They do not hire or fire their employees as other institutions do, because not all their employees are employed as people are everywhere else. They do not draw their talent from uniform pools in the society, nor are they meant to, nor should they. When colleges and universities are treated by others as if they were like any of these other organizations, they complain—bitterly, brilliantly—but they have a difficult time explaining. Of course, they are themselves by no means all alike, even though they look like nothing else.

In dealing with private colleges and universities (and with the rest of the not-for-profit sector), government can and does deal by analogy with other parts of our industrial society. But these analogies spring only from bureaucratic necessity, not from intimate experience, and they often do not work. Thus the reality: while private (and public) institutions of higher education become one of the most heavily regulated parts of American society, they gnaw at the hand that feeds them more and more, and more and more are they repelled by the implications of their needs. Thus their dilemma: believing they must remind the young, and the nation, of larger concerns than simply the self, they embrace contradiction and plead, scold and threaten more and more for themselves. They become the nodes of self-interest they inveigh against. You are, of course, watching it happen at this moment, and it is neither a pretty sight nor a pleasant sensation.

The government in a democracy ought to communicate its limits. A free society must not wish to over-control the very process by which its young learn how valuable and irreplaceable its freedoms— of merit competing, of choice and belief and speech —are. The process by which those values and others are learned is the educational process, and that process has a deep and abiding purpose, which government shares and should not wish to deter; namely, the shaping of citizens.

I say that because I believe that the formation of a

basis for how we choose to believe and speak and treat others—how, in short, we choose a civic role for ourselves—is the basic purpose of an education in a democracy. The content, the data, the information, of schooling can be anything in the wide world. But the purpose of education, as opposed to information, is to lead us to some sense of citizenship, to some shared assumptions about individual freedoms and institutional needs, to some sense of the full claims of self as they are to be shared with others. For some, I may have a much too old-fashioned sense of the civic claims of education and an insufficient regard for the social claims. But I would argue that without an ethically-based civic sense, nourished in an individual through education, larger social claims issue merely into programs for action with no controlling perspective about what the action is for. Action without a deeper purpose is useless; it is only activity, and that is always finally susceptible to the sweet, solipsistic allure of anarchy. Historically, education has been the best stay against such confusion, by fostering the civilizing ability to make choices and to act responsibly for others on the basis of those choices.

I think it is critical to reaffirm the civic goal of an education and the way that goal is attained through choice in the educational process. It is important to say again that through individual choices, not by slogans or shibboleths or shamanistic incantation, we become engaged in common concerns. It is im-

8

portant to say it now, I believe, because now powerful forces press young people and their parents and schools in a quite opposite direction: away from an education concerned at heart with ethical choice and civic effort and toward a view of schooling as immediately, intensely, insistently useful.

I am not alone in feeling everywhere a deep ache to redefine everything in terms that serve only the self rather than in terms that shape the self with a civic sense for others. Much of this mood derives from the straitened economic conditions in the country, conditions that only encourage in young people (and in their parents) the need to define at the beginning of adult lives an ultimate vocation. This grinding and pressing vocationalism is not the students' fault; they hear nothing else from parents or national leaders or any of the rest of us but of the hard times ahead and of how bleak it looks and how the dollar plunges and unemployment soars and, as the century winds down and the millennium nears, of how many promises have been broken and how the glass of all our hopes is shattered. As these students remember the battles of their older siblings in the 1960s, over telephones, in living rooms, by mail, on police blotters, in emergency rooms, they resolve not to cause that kind of family civil war or bear the scars in their genes and generation; and as places like Yale (and others) break past $10,000 a year for the privilege of working hard and competing harder, they look at a younger brother or sister who will not even dream of such a place unless indebtedness is to become as ingrained in the middle class as self-loathing is.

The vocationalism, the urge to be professional early so as to have something later, is lamentable, understandable and manageable. There is no point in making students feel guilty about it, or in pretending that work in the world is beneath them, or in flaying today's student because he is not yesterday's, living in a van in Vermont. The vocationalism is not necessarily either wrong or foolish—*if* its pragmatism can be aimed, *if* that pragmatism can be attached to a purpose and that purpose to other people in some substantial way, and to larger purposes. The dangerous and debilitating vocationalism is the one that higher education, fearing for survival, is tempted to pander to rather than to pattern: a vocationalism that is merely self-regarding, that only narrows someone at eighteen down to anxiety about a job, that leaves him or her only with ambition but no affiliations. That vocationalism strangles the power of choice in the name of necessity and cripples the urge to a flexible civic sense when that sense ought to be gathering soundness and strength. Such a willful vocationalism, urged on the young person so early and often, lacks the capacious spirit through which one might freely educate oneself for a life of some benefit to others.

It is that vision of self, in precisely the least promising of times, that educational institutions, at whatever level, must assert again, for they, like government, ought to assert their limits. It must be said that school cannot save all souls, cannot serve all the needs of society, cannot do everything that governments and churches and families and strong traditions must also do. But, in the least promising of times, schools, especially institutions of higher education, can affirm that there is no specialization in a democracy unless there is first a broad, deep base of shared assumptions and perceptions, growing out of a carefully wrought curriculum, about where we have come from and what that pluralism of values and backgrounds and peoples had as a purpose, and how important is the unity in and through that diversity. While it may feel as if we are reinventing the wheel at a time when everyone wants to go by Concorde, it is precisely now that the values, and value, of a liberal education must be asserted again, a liberal education whose intellectual core is a required curriculum and whose purpose is the development of students who can make rational, humane, informed choices, and citizens.

In the teeth of the forces that buffet them, private universities must assert again what they are: how they embody the principle of collaborative effort, how they are built of affiliations, of courses and appointments and research efforts and values. They must communicate to others their nature, which is their connectedness within and their complex connections without. They must assert their fragility and toughness, their combination of susceptibility to every seismic quiver in the society and their insist-

11

ence that they determine for themselves what quality is and how it is tested and tried and proven. Private universities cannot be diffident about their artificial, curiously hierarchical nature or their essentially intellectual and civic purpose. They must be able to persuade others that the ability to pursue the truth responsibly and freely is a precious charge and a national asset and that responsibility and freedom are not incompatible desires or goals. Universities must be able to explain how they are part of a larger vision a society must set for itself—of a mutually supportive and candidly respectful culture where pluralism is ordered so that it can be nourished and where diversity is defined as a good. Universities cannot believe, lest they lie to themselves, that they alone contain this vision, but they cannot be forced to compromise their vision, lest society lose one of its central modes for seeing.

A government's needs to impose responsibility and a university's need to inquire freely must exist together in a complex, delicate and trustful balance; government and private universities must learn about each other's needs and natures in order not to maul and manipulate each other. If quality is to be maintained for the country's good, then there must be recognition on both parts that neither part gains from forcing the other to its mold or model.

There is another form of recognition that must also occur, and that takes me back to where I began. At the outset I asserted that survival would force private universities, particularly with regard to the government, to become a new special-interest group, and I said that need would contravene something deep in their natures. In fact, neither public government nor private institutions can exist for or sustain narrowly defined special interest. In fact, governmental and educational institutions, and the processes they stand for, are meant to serve, in different ways, the same public interest and public trust and, in fact, both kinds of institutions choke on special pressures. We share not only an ironic relationship but a much larger common problem, which is how to deal with the country's rush to define issues only in terms of constituencies rather than in terms of commonalities.

There is in America a retreat from structures of mutuality to strategies for special accommodation, and neither government nor education, neither agencies nor universities, can survive by simply spinning off special solutions or by making themselves into a special-interest group. Any institution that responds only to localized, political pressure and not to broader claims of civic principle splits its polity and fragments itself.

America is in danger of overloading its political system, and hence, in ways we have not yet fully realized, its various educational systems. It asks each to bear too much. The political system, where competing needs must be recognized and assessed, cannot function when every need presents itself as an

13

Absolute Imperative and thus refuses to recognize that other claims could possibly compete. Such a spirit of absolutism renders the political system incapable of the civilizing flexibility that a democracy needs. And when that spirit of special, as opposed to public, interest enters the campuses, a different system is just as incapacitated. The educational system's instincts for equity and the educational institution's collaborative structure are threatened at their core.

A private education must be in some form directed to the public good, and nothing is gained from assuming that private universities and colleges do not want to, or cannot, fulfill that purpose. A private university meets its social obligations by giving young people of ability from the widest possible variety of backgrounds and energies and talents the opportunity to educate themselves and to be educated for the full claims of citizenship. The self-reliance of such institutions and individuals must be encouraged, not eroded. Private universities must be nourished in order that they may continue to be tributaries to the great stream of American culture and not forced to become sanctuaries from it. Rather than assuming that the private sector, including universities, is incapable of assuming a civic role, it is in everyone's interest to listen and learn from each other and to cherish the powerful pluralism, and all it implies, that is the unique instinct and strength of our country.

I said I intended neither to petition nor to promulgate. I rather propose. The proposition is a simple

14

one: that it is finally in the public interest that we, government and university, serve that interest as generously and supportively as possible, and that means understanding each other's particular mission and respecting the different paths to a common end.

The Nature and Purpose of the University

We at Yale have never been stronger. In the last twenty-five years, under three Presidents, the University has steadily grown in the depth of its faculty, the diversity of its students, and its commitment to equity in its daily processes. Under Presidents Griswold, Brewster and Gray, Yale has become a truly international university, its affiliations through scholarship and students reaching all over the globe, its men and women drawn from every part of America, its ancient purpose, inscribed in a New England town, now a banner flown everywhere. And when the country needed a standard in times of uncertainty and disaffection, it found it at Yale, where the courageous stewardship of Kingman Brewster reminded a university of its heritage of ordered openness and thus kept it free.

16

The Nature and Purpose of the University

A civilized order is the precondition of freedom, and freedom—of belief, speech and choice—the goal of responsible order. A university cannot expound those goals and expect a larger society to find them compelling, it cannot become a repository of national hope and a source of national leadership, unless it strives to practice what it teaches. If its goals are noble, so must be its acts.

The American university constantly challenges the capacity of individuals to associate in a spirit of free inquiry, with a decent respect for the opinion of others. Its values are those of free, rational and humane investigation and behavior. Its faith, constantly renewed and ever vulnerable, holds that if its values are sufficiently respected within, their growth will be encouraged without. Its purpose is to teach those who wish to learn, learn from those it teaches, foster research and original thought, and, through its students and faculty, to disseminate knowledge and to transmit values of responsible civic and intellectual behavior. That purpose can never become the captive of any single ideology or dogma. Nor can it be taken for granted.

In its purpose, the University embodies the pluralistic spirit of America, and it embodies that spirit in another way as well. The country's promise that diverse peoples, with diverse origins and goals, can compete on the basis of merit for the fulfillment of their aspirations, is also the basic premise of the University's composition. But while the University engages the best hopes and, at various stages, the

17

ablest people of the larger society, it does not pretend in every respect to be a microcosm of the larger society. While it has democratized its values, it has not in every sense made its structure democratic. The University's structure is a hierarchy unlike any other; it is neither military nor corporate; nor is it even a hierarchy like the Church whence sprang the earliest University teachers. With its instincts for collaboration and its strategies for consultation, the University is finally a patient and persuasive hierarchy, designed to cherish a particular value-laden process and the individuals within it. That process is, of course, the educational process, wherein the individual, often alone, often with others, seeks constantly to clarify limits in order to surpass them, constantly seeks to order the mind so as to set it free. That seeking is the University's essence.

Intellectual and civic in nature, pluralistic in purpose and composition, hierarchical in structure, the University exists for that play of restraint and release in each of its individual members. Through that creative play of opposites in teaching, learning and research, the University nourishes at its core the humanizing and spacious acts of the individual imagination. Those acts are found in every area of study, whether lasers, literature or law, and are proof of the human capacity to make and to impose a design. Those designs made by the imagination are the signs of our ability to shape instinct and flux, to find or reveal patterns in the seemingly unplanned. The University is the guardian of the imagination

18

that both defines and asserts our humanity.

The University is not only the guardian of that human capacity, it is also its triumph. For as the University is devoted to fostering these individual acts of imagination, so the University is an imaginative act in itself. In its mixed structure, its assertions about itself, its mingled character as a force for change and a wellspring of continuity, the University is in a sense self-consciously artificial. The University is something made, not born, cradling those individual acts of shaping that it figures forth. It is our culture's assertion that what is made by the mind has value and can convey values. Thus the University, rooted in history, open to every new impulse, insists on its centrality to culture and on its uniqueness. Thus it is so powerful and so fragile, the foe of the merely random, insistent on order while urging freedom, convinced that the human mind, out of nature, can fashion shapes and patterns nature never bore, and convinced that it is prime among the artifacts.

Where universities, or those within them, falter is in believing that the formal nature of the University, what I have called its artificial character, necessarily removes them and their inhabitants from the common stream of society; that because universities assert the mind's capacity, in the best sense, to contrive, they can condescend to or smugly disdain whatever is not encompassed by them. Such an attitude has brought many institutions the scorn they deserve, for they have chosen to be sanctuaries from

19

society and not tributaries to it. To wish only to be removed from the culture, and not to be part of its renewal, is to long for the atrophy, not the exercise, of the imagination and its works. I return to where I began—no university is strong if it is unsure of its purpose and nature, and is unwilling or unable to make vital that nature and purpose for others beyond it. We lose our public trust when we treat as only private our principal obligations.

Only when we clarify what we believe are the larger values, and value, of a private education can we expect that education to have a significant effect for the public good. I began by speaking of Yale's strength. But our strength is not simply our numbers and our variety and our quality. Our basic strength derives from our common sense of what we do, why we do it, and whom we mean to reach.

Our strength also derives from our capacity to know where our problems will occur. While no Sybil has yet vouchsafed me certain knowledge of the future, even one unencumbered by special vision can see the outlines of our path. Let me review what is perhaps known to all here, and then speak of some particular challenges before us.

Earlier this fall I had occasion to note a mood of closure and withdrawal that seems to be growing around us. I sense more than the contraction and spasm of isolation that would inevitably follow a period as expansive as the sixties and an experience as searing as the war in Vietnam. This mood of disaffiliation has these roots and others as well and it casts a longer shadow. We are coming to the end of the twentieth century, and the knowledge we bear weighs heavily. Part of our knowledge is the realization that systems, technological and ideological, in which we had such faith, have their limits, that we may have reached those limits and that we are being left with only the fragments of our hopes. We are closing not only a century but also a millennium, and the accumulated force of that realization heightens a certain apocalyptic impulse, a febrile fatigue. As if to accommodate this spirit and contain it, the country seems to want to settle only for a credible competence in its education, its government, its means of pleasure, its craftsmanship. It should never want less, but it ought to aspire to more, and universities and colleges must have the will and the energy to focus themselves, and the nation, on renewal despite the entropy that a sense of closure creates. Because the next years in our enterprise of education will be difficult, because nothing one can see will make them easy, our faith in ourselves and our courage to do what we believe in must be all the stronger. Let me be specific.

General economic conditions, specifically a corrosive inflation, will place educational institutions, with their concentrations of people, increasingly on the defensive. These institutions will be harder pressed than ever to retain their levels of financial aid, to keep tuitions from escalating at anything less than the national rate of inflation, to compensate those who work in them at levels commensurate with their skills. And those assaults of a fiscal nature will only be abetted by inevitable demographic curves. Within a dozen years there will be just about a million fewer eighteen-year-olds in America than there were three years ago. The competition for potential college applicants will increase dramatically, and no institution will be immune. For even those universities whose colleges will still attract a greater pool of applicants than there will be places in a class, will feel this shrinkage because their doctoral candidates will find, as so many are now finding, that there is no market for their skills. Indeed, of all the immediate challenges facing the major research universities—to sustain research libraries, to support academic science in the context of a university population that will shrink, to plan the direction of medical education, to finance graduate students and to embrace part-time or older students in new patterns—the most difficult and internally consequential will be the need to attract into the academic profession the ablest and most dedicated young men and women. Nothing we do in colleges or universities or that the country wants done is possible without the next generation of teachers and scholars. I will return to this concern.

In the years ahead of us, precisely because the pressures on private institutions, whether large or small, old or new, will increase, it will be essential to affirm the particular character of private institu-

22

tions and to remember that because times are financially strained, the government is not always the place to turn for help. Such rescue, even if it were to occur, would result in more regulation. Of course we depend on federal funds for a wide variety of crucial research and financial aid; of course there are legitimate requirements of accountability for the taxpayers' dollars that follow federal funds; of course there are legitimate regulatory functions of the federal government. But the capacity of a private institution to choose for itself what its course will be, in keeping with the law of the land, is essential to its nature and purpose, and we must be constantly wary of governmental intrusion and of asking for or accepting more. We must retain our freedom of expression and of purpose.

Private educational institutions, however, must not only resist external interference. They must realize they are an integral part of the private sector, and other portions of the private sector must also come to this realization. As I have had occasion to say, the ancient ballet of mutual antagonism—at times evidently so deeply satisfying—between private enterprise, on the one hand, and private education, on the other, is not to anyone's interest. That ballet of antagonism must give way to a capacity for responsible collaboration. There is a metaphor that informs the private business sector as it informs the private educational sector, and that is the metaphor of the free marketplace. Whether the competition of the free marketplace is of commodities or of ideas, it is a common metaphor and a precious asset.

Obviously I am not asking to resist governmental intrusion in order to encourage or accept intrusion of any other kind from any other quarter. What I am saying is that precisely to retain our capacity to choose, and to survive as we wish to survive as a private institution, Yale, and places like Yale, must recognize their natural alliances with other private institutions. Such alliances must spring from a perception that all portions of the private sector—voluntary, corporate, and educational—have a common goal, in a pluralistic society, of providing alternatives to public structures and solutions.

Lastly, and this is less a problem than a challenge, we must be mindful of the community in which we live. No college or university in a city can regard its fortunes as separate from that city. The economic and cultural health of New Haven is intimately tied to Yale's health, and our future is intertwined with New Haven's. The City and the University share the same ground and over two hundred and fifty years of history. Yale cannot look at New Haven as if the City were an endless impediment, and New Haven cannot regard Yale as a smugly unresponsive savior. Neither attitude reflects reality, and the only attitude that will reflect reality is one of mutual regard and collaboration. The University must do all it can to assist the City in its development, and in those ways that it legitimately can, it will. The City must also understand that Yale's resources are limited and that Yale's first obligation is to fulfill itself as an educational institution. If Yale falters in that, the City cannot flourish. Those who chide Yale for not being primarily an agency of specific, local reforms in fact misapprehend the University's nature and purpose. That misapprehension in part is Yale's fault, but misapprehensions, of all kinds, should be dispelled if our common future is to be shaped in common.

And what are the prime imperatives for Yale's future? I think they are three:

First, Yale must use its financial and human resources prudently, imaginatively and wisely. We must affirm those internal affiliations, among the Schools, among the Schools and the College, among Departments, that will focus on critical strengths and encourage new patterns of teaching and research to emerge. We will not be able to do everything, but what we choose to do we must do well. The purpose of the next years of budgetary contraction is to consolidate in order to preserve excellence and to maintain Yale's finest tradition— the offering of a private education for the public good. We cannot blink at the need to live within our means, but budgetary balance can and must be achieved in a way that enhances our quality, not in a way that sacrifices our quality.

Second, Yale must continue to reflect and nourish the pluralism of America. I take the diversity in this country—of peoples, of kinds of freedoms and of humane and rational values—to be both a source of the country's strength and a vital principle in itself. To be truly a national institution, playing its educational and civic role to the fullest, Yale's texture can never be less varied and many-grained than the fabric of America itself. If Yale is to train leaders, they must come from and respond to every part of the larger society. This heterogeneity of talent and origin, experience and interest, is not achievable by simple formulae or by institutionalizing special privilege. It is done by continually seeking out, as students and faculty and staff, men and women of merit with a capacity to contribute to the fulfillment of themselves and hence of the place, and by continually urging and encouraging them to become part of Yale. This affirmative attitude is translated into action by our never wavering in our commitment to seek out these individuals as widely and diligently as possible.

Third, and I return to and close with a concern expressed earlier, Yale must expend every effort to nourish and encourage its young or nontenured faculty. The University must demonstrate its belief in them and their efforts. If it does not, it cannot expect younger faculty to believe in the institution or in their vocation. That vocation, the academic profession, and the younger teacher and scholar, most particularly in the humanities and certain social sciences, are now subjected to the savage pressures I noted earlier, the declining numbers of students, soaring costs, and diminishing number of jobs. And,

I respectfully suggest, these pressures are only exacerbated by state legislation* that, in Connecticut, has recently denied private institutions the capacity to determine for themselves when faculty must retire. Here a governmental act, however well intentioned in its specific mission, has a devastating effect in areas clearly not envisaged by its proponents. With no age limit for faculty in private educational institutions, the private and public institutions are set at odds; the capacity of individuals and institutions to plan ahead is confounded at a critical time; the young person is placed in a hopeless position, with no sense of movement within and diminishing chances without. Finally, if one cannot recruit young faculty of quality, and give them some hope, there is a serious threat to our capacity to fulfill the human and moral principles of pluralism expressed in programs of affirmative action.

There are, of course, measures one can take and my concern for the younger faculty in no way bespeaks a lack of regard for the older faculty. I use this example as a way of describing how so many of my concerns—about excellence, about resources, about diversity, about the character of a private institution—intersect in issues concerning the faculty, and particularly concerning our young colleagues. I believe the faculty is at the heart of this place, and I believe that at the heart of the faculty in a place like Yale is the teaching function. All the research we want to do, all the obligations we must

* Repealed in 1979.

carry as faculty, are in some sense nurtured by and are versions of that first calling, which is to teach our students. We want always to do more, but we can never do less. Nor can we ever forget that.

Surely, all of us can recall certain voices, the voices of teachers who changed the way we live our lives. I am concerned, at last, with the next generation of voices. I wish them to be as strong and confident and effective in what they do as those who came before. And they will be, if we recall our nature and our purpose and engage each other to fashion our future together.

The Apocalyptic Style

Doubtless through the spring and summer you experienced some doubts. Any rational person would. In the bower of anyone contemplating the fact of beginning college there must be some creeping tendril of anxiety, some late summer's night when the inner ear heard the inner voice ask—What is the point to it all? And will anyone tell me or am I expected to know?

You are not supposed to know but you are expected to wish to know. And I am expected to tell you. Indeed, in examining the purpose of what you now begin, you begin to do what you are here to do; you begin to examine assumptions, hone your powers of analysis, expand your capacities for synthesis. You begin to grow out of yourselves and into us, whoever us is. In the words of a famous report on education of the Yale College faculty in 1828, you are here to be thrown upon the resources of your own mind. And that means defining and refining those resources by drawing upon the resources of the place and of the other people in the place. To what end? So that the individual mind and spirit, made civil and capacious and curious, can foster the good and the knowledge it wishes for itself on behalf of others. The ultimate goal is to make the one, through fulfillment of the self, part of the many.

You have come to a great, ancient University and to the College within it in an even older New England city on the water. You are not the first, nor will you be the last, to come with your questions. The questions you ask yourself and will ask of Yale, and that the times will ask you, are natural and appropriate. No one ought to approach an education or a university in a spirit which is settled or unquestioning or smug or certain of answers or results. Intellectual curiosity, a hunger for contact with the wider world as it is aggregated here, a desire to test one's best with others, all of that is the very spirit Yale would encourage in you if Yale did not find it in you. You are in the right place.

You have also come not only to a great, ancient university but to a place marked with its origins as a puritan village. If you come here, therefore, questioning your election, that too is still in the spirit of the place. You will know you are truly of Yale as well as at it when you hear yourself indulging in that oldest puritan pastime—talking about how hard you work. One of the deepest pleasures of this place is to spend leisure time expostulating about work. Futile as it may be to resist a deep institutional tide that began to flow hereabouts in October 1701, I will assert in passing that pleasure can derive as much from contemplation as from activity, as much from thinking about what you are doing as from being busy at it.

I raise the questions of your natural anxieties and the need for some larger sense of purpose, of the puritan origins of this place, and of America, and of the inevitable call to busyness and frantic activity those origins imply, because such concerns are part of a much larger set of concerns in our country to-day—concerns about pace, anxiety about purpose, questions of capacity and coherence. I speak to these anxieties because you will have to learn to manage them, here and later, and because I can better say what our purpose is if that purpose, at Yale, is in perspective.

The 1980s are here and, that fictional boundary now crossed, the pace of anxiety quickens. In the West we have a particular accounting system whereby we measure and make manageable duration. We create what we call time, among other ways, in multiples of ten—decades, centuries, millennia. These deep, and deeply important, fictions represent boundaries we set ourselves. When we cross them, we revive our sense of advancement. All cultures

31

set a starting date for the present era, a point of origin, a year one. In the movement away from that point of beginning across more and more boundaries, there is a paradox: whatever moment is newest is also oldest, for today is older than all the yesterdays; whatever moment is oldest is youngest, for whatever was a thousand years ago is also, in retrospect, younger. Priority always belongs to the "primitive"; modernity is what is most aged. We must recognize, therefore, that advancement also means accumulation—of fatigue and failure as much as innovation and "progress."

When we give ourselves these fresh starts every ten years, or every hundred years, or even, once before, every thousand years, we are giving ourselves the necessary illusion that we have breasted a tape and won a race, even though the marathon continues as it always has, regardless of the little stops for breath we allow ourselves to make. The long run is made bearable only by all the short runs. Now, at the outset of the 1980s, we are beginning another short run.

Across a century, however, these sprints of a decade tire the race. The accumulated heaviness wears as we all look back at the last hundred years. The consciousness of this accumulation and the sense of decline it engenders led, at the end of the last century, to the coining of the phrase *fin de siècle*, the phrase implying decadence, that is, lack of vitality and softness of effort in the face of demands of the world. That accumulated fear of decline and hunger for hope is strong at the end of centuries and strongest at the end of ten centuries, or a millennium. Then we hear most clearly the accent of the Apocalypse.

That accent derives from many sources but one of the most piercing expressions of mingled promise and terror is in the final book of the Bible, the Revelation given to Saint John on the Isle of Patmos. In the twentieth chapter we hear that an angel comes down and binds the serpent for a thousand years, and in those thousand years Christ reigns with those who believed in Him. But when that millennium expires, Satan is loosed out of his prison for a little season, and that season is one of war, deception and fire, until the second time, when God opens His book, the book of life, says John, and all are judged by that book according to their works, and whosoever is not found written there is cast into a lake of fire. And that, says John, is the second and final death.

This terrifying and exhilarating vision, so important to the culture of seventeenth-century England that shaped America in its origins, leaves its mark. It leaves its mark in the details of the Apocalypse, still the details of any version of the end anyone holds down deep. It leaves its mark in the larger prophecy that complete closure comes, and that it will come in terms of a thousand years, and bring seasons of hope and disaster until some are saved and some are not. Given this hectic and indelible vision, it is small wonder that perhaps 980 years ago, more or less, masses of people in Europe thought the world was

going to end; small wonder that the third term of ten
—a millennium—reinforces our sense of the reality
of the first term of ten—a decade; small wonder,
alas, that the coercive rhetoric of the Apocalypse
never seems to lose its allure, and parts of us—whatever
our beliefs—respond to the trumpet of Armageddon despite the voice of reason.

All this is preamble to where we think we are,
beginning a new decade, beginning the end of a century,
ending the second millennium. Humankind
becomes more consciously retrospective the more it
fears the seemingly uncontrollable accumulation of
the past, and so it is with us. Throughout the Western
world, the decline of the West is feared, and that
fear feeds itself. In America, self-consciousness is
acute, and keen is our sense of anxiety about our advancing
accumulation of responsibility and failed
effort. We hear on all sides that we are weak; that
knowledge is exploding unmanageably; that the pace
of uncontrollable events is exacerbated by instantaneous
communication; that technology is a beast
biting its own tail; that ideology is insufficient to an
exploding reality; that the family is in decline; that
traditional values are devalued; that standards, for
work and play and quality of life, are gone.

I believe the new wisdom of a century's end is
really only fatigue masquerading as philosophy. I
urge you to beware the captivation of these easy,
thoughtless profundities. These banalities have only
in common the belief that we are not able to give
definition—shape and contour—to what is around

34

us. These shibboleths finally tell more about those who utter them than about reality. They are expressions of exhaustion more often than they are forms of explanation. They tell us that when the pressure of accounting for everything within living memory becomes overwhelming, the desire to control is matched, and often mastered, by a profound sense of a loss of control.

At such moments, what power consists of and who will have it become pressing questions. They become more pressing because autonomy and the capacity to define the contour of events, to seize Fortune by the forelock, are threatened. The inevitable reaction to powerlessness, including knowing what power is and what it is for, is to react the way we see so many in this country reacting: it is to retreat into self-interest, to hunker down, to isolate the society, to make all public concerns matters of private prerogative, so that the hunched individual can find compensation for his sense of thwarted autonomy in the public realm. In our country we see a deeply dangerous turning away from public obligations that is the result of a dangerous turning in to find sufficiency where it finally is not—only in the self. We are urged to isolate ourselves as a nation, to erect walls of tariff or trade or arms; to question all strategies for collaboration and alliance and to embrace only tactics of self-satisfying accommodation. We are urged to solve moral problems by decree, and to grow weary of processes of the law. Such are the counsels of the tired short run.

Ethnic groups divide and collide, religious communities seize fads as if they were faiths, political processes undergo changes in institutional shape only teasingly and superficially signaled by the cynicism of a free electorate. Within these cultural and religious and political contexts, we are assured by those with the obligation to lead that nothing has worked as promised, and promises have no ability to work. Promises are not made or viewed as enduring institutions but only as expedient impulses. All of what is said in this Apocalyptic Style rushes us past the processes of public reason to the self-lacerating counsels of private despair. And this rush to unreason is nowhere clearer than in our public speech, the speech our society uses for itself, the speech public leaders, of whatever kind, use to set a national mood or establish a sense of purpose. You can tell a great deal about a people's stability and confidence from the way it talks to and about itself in public. In this country now, seized by the Apocalyptic Style, everything is overstated because overstatement is meant to redeem our feeling of being overwhelmed. Whether the rhetoric is for or against nuclear power, or for or against registration for the draft, or for or against a religious or political party, the rhetoric is often coercive, pandering to fear rather than appealing to reason, summoning the specter of the end of the world rather than pausing to examine the world, within and without, as it must be lived in.

America is a religious nation without a coherent creed, a believing people hungering for a faith to which to give its assent. So much of what passes for moral certitude today covers a void but does not fill it. The void remains. But that is not yet the Apocalypse. Divisions and problems there are. But Armageddon is not yet. The race has a long, long way to go. What seems exhausted to many is not; it is they who are tired. The frenzy that sees the End at every moment sees an illusion. My message is simple: so much of what you will hear, during your time here and later, springs from a fatigue and failure of nerve that would ensnare you and your strength in its weakness. Beware it; do not be charmed by it. Do not become one of those who have only the courage of other people's convictions. Be one of those who believe in what Shakespeare called the pauser, reason. Be one for whom coercion, of any kind, whether coercion based on race or sex or religious or political belief, is an anathema. Leave the Apocalyptic Style to those who cannot, or do not want to, do the deeply human work of finding their own voices in the common chorus.

New decade; end of a century; millennium; the fact is, nothing is old or tired or declining for you. You are new. You do not need only the worn intellectual cloaks of others; you must weave your own, with which to walk out in the world. That is why you are here, to grow in intellectual capacity, human sensitivity, spiritual depth, through the process— begun here, life-long in duration—of a liberal education. A liberal education is not an education for the impractical; it is the intensely practical act of self-fashioning that occurs as you develop your intellectual and human powers across a variety of areas of intellectual inquiry and methods and values. The purpose of this self-fashioning is not to get a job; it is to develop yourself, so that whatever you do later will not be done from a narrow or parochial human base. The larger purpose of this self-fashioning is to learn how to turn the self out, to reach into yourself so as to reach beyond yourself—out to others, in order to make a country, and the lives of your fellow citizens, better.

A liberal education is a process of self-knowledge for the purpose of shared civility. It should foster a skepticism of the apocalyptic or coercive style, a tolerance for other beliefs and peoples, a passion for excellence and equity, a respect for the dignity of the individual. Such an education begins in Yale College but should not end here; it is not a product, freeze-dried and wrapped in a plastic bag, that you "get" by attendance in class or grades or by acts of faculty and trustees; it has nothing to do with credentials or accreditation or profession. A liberal education is a process, whereby we each make ourselves part of a commonality that respects the majesty and integrity of the individual talent. To engage the process you have only to embrace the proposition that by testing yourself against the new you will be made, by yourself, renewed.

I welcome you to the manifold pleasures of the spirit of renaissance.

Sentimentality

Today's college students [1975]—the former grammar and high school students of the late 1960s and early 1970s—have lost touch with the language. These were the children nobody remembered when The Movement was moving, when the rest of us were being liberated. These were the genuine young.

They are the products of the anti-structures of that time. They have come and are coming out of the open classroom, vertical grouping, modular buildings with fifty pupils to a room. They have come out of the new math and its concepts, its Legos and blocks and set theory, not knowing how to multiply. They have come out of individualized instruction and elective systems, not knowing how to listen to anyone else, not knowing how to take a direction.

They have come out of the sentimental 1960s,

when "repressive" and "arbitrary" grades were done away with, not able to take the pressure of grading. They have come out of a primary and secondary world where personal development was said to be worth more than achievement, where creativity was the highest goal and was often completely divorced from one of its essential components: discipline. And they are arriving in college often completely at a loss about how to cope with their work, with their time, with themselves.

But most of all, these present college students, and those now in junior high and high school, cannot handle the English language, particularly as it is written.

That this is so is no secret. The *New York Times* recently reported that in the ten years since 1964 the verbal and math scores on the scholastic achievement tests (SATs) have been steadily declining, and that the average test scores for 1975 high school graduates declined by ten points on the verbal portion and by eight points on the math portion since 1974. This was the largest single drop in the past twelve years.

This decline tells us something real and terrifying about the state of the English language, just as a recent article on course enrollments in foreign languages in the *Chronicle of Higher Education* tells us something about literacy and the state of foreign languages. The Modern Language Association reports a drop of 6.2 percent in undergraduate enrollments in foreign languages from 1972 to 1974, with sharpest declines of 14 percent in German, 13.4 percent in French, 11.6 percent in Russian, and slighter declines in Italian and Spanish. This, the article said, reflects a trend that has been apparent since the late 1960s.

Obviously the inclination to immerse oneself in any language is on the wane, and the ability to *use* language is withering rapidly. Ask anyone who reads student writing—or hires recent graduates. Last fall the Yale English Department voted to reinstate English 10, a composition course, because so many Yale students cannot handle English—cannot make a sentence or a paragraph, cannot organize a paper, cannot follow through—well enough to do college work.

Yale is not unique. To take a university different in every respect except quality, Berkeley has just created the Bay Area Writing Project, bringing together college, junior college and high school teachers in the San Francisco area to work on each other to work on student writing. Why? Because where seven years ago only about 25 percent of Berkeley students had to take Subject A, Berkeley's required basic composition course for entering freshmen, now the number is around 50 percent. Berkeley saw the quality of writing declining sharply and decided to invest its energies in the students' earlier years by going back into the high schools. From the Free Speech Movement to the Bay Area Writing Project in just ten years.

Never mind the statistics. Ask the students. They

will tell you how badly they need help with their language. Last year at Yale, 185 students applied for twelve places in one small college seminar on expository writing—nothing fancy, just a course on how to write. This is typical of the students' desperate wish to be taught how to handle the fundamental medium in which we live.

What has happened? I believe that of all the institutions attacked in the past dozen years—governmental, legal and educational—the one that suffered most was the institution of language itself, that massive, living system of signs which on the one hand limits us and, on the other hand, allows us to decide who we are. This institution—language—was perceived as being repressive. It was thought to be the agent of all other repressive codes—legal, political and cultural. Language was the barrier that blocked —blocked access to pure feeling, blocked true communal experience of the kind that flowered at Woodstock, blocked the restoration of Eden.

Language was what was circumvented by drugs and music—those agents of higher states whose main virtue was that they were not verbal but visual or aural, the pure association of pure shape or sound unencumbered by words—which is to say by distinctions, which is to say by meaning. Language disassociated us from primitive impulses. It polluted us with ambiguity; it was not pure. Language impeded freedom.

Sentimentality

The first shot in the revolution in 1964 was the Filthy Speech Movement. It was intended not only to free speech from middle-class constraints, about uttering obscenities, for instance. It was also intended to free us from the shackles of syntax, the racism of grammar, the elitism of style. All those corrupt and corrupting elements in American society, those signs that we had fallen from paradise, could be located in an aspect of language. The Filthy Speech Movement was where we first began to hear language mediated through the bullhorn into the formulaic chant of a crowd.

This reductiveness would soon be extended to all kinds of systems that asserted differentness or pluralism as essential to their workings. But language was where it was first applied. The slogan, like the picket sign, the bumper sticker, the single name by which so many people in The Movement went (surnames being invidious)—all were part of an effort to compress language to a single unambiguous medium of exchange, a coin of the realm that could not be counterfeited or abused. What was being sought was not the protean leap of language, but unity of feeling—complete integration of desire and fulfillment.

And here is where language was more of an enemy than anything else. For while language may be a medium for sentimentality, it will not finally yield to it. Try as you can, you can neither wholly avoid words nor wholly make them mean only what you feel. Words resist. But Abbie Hoffman said it better than I can. I quote from Hoffman's speech on the warm evening of May 1, 1970, in the courtyard of Ezra Stiles College at Yale, on the occasion of one of the last great campus gatherings of The Movement:

"Don't listen to people who say we got to be serious, responsible. Everybody's responsible and serious but us. We gotta redefine the ———— language. Work —W–O–R–K—is a dirty four-letter word. . . . We need a society in which work and play are not separate. We gotta destroy the Protestant ethic as well as capitalism, racism, imperialism—that's gotta go too. We want a society in which dancin' in the streets isn't separate from cuttin' sugar cane. . . . We have picked the Yale lock."

Fascinating. Because the Protestant ethic, capitalism, racism and imperialism are almost forgotten, almost mere afterthoughts, as Hoffman proclaimed what he really wants: a garden world where nothing is separate, work and play, cutting cane and dancing, where the togetherness will come by "redefining the language." If only he could redefine the language as easily as he could manipulate a crowd. But language won't change its essential shape for anyone. If you engage it, you must honor its deep tides. The most that Abbie Hoffman can do is make it do tricks, and the pun at the end is his trick.

Abbie Hoffman's attitude to language was fundamentally sentimental—language was a medium for expressing his feelings. It wasn't really a rhetorical instrument, to be used to persuade others, or a weapon, used to flay others. It was like everything else to him and to those like him—good as long as it made you feel good.

This sentimentality, corrosive as acid, was true of all those for whom books became talismans and fetishes, helpful for inducing states and sensations. This is how the novels of Herman Hesse, awash in sentiment, were used, and those of Kurt Vonnegut, Jr. Vonnegut was a culture hero because he seemed to be grinning through exquisite pain, the result of his extraordinary moral sensitivity. As Robert Alter has suggested, the young loved his sense of resignation and the fact that his America was glistening with corruption and guilt and failure. They also loved him because his zany cartoons masqueraded as tragic complexities and therefore massaged their prejudices without requiring them to think. This was the perfect writer for people who felt that words were crowding them, impeding them: people for whom Zen, the occult, Indians, organic gardening, transcendental meditation, the I Ching—the whole frozen dinner of the new primitivism—were superior to words.

The only texts to be trusted were Eastern ones that might lead to trance or offered no resistance to it. This accounts for the prodigious sales of that poisonous sweetmeat, *The Prophet*, by Kahlil Gibran. For, like Rod McKuen, Gibran continued to satisfy the sentimental longings for absorption of those for whom real politics or drugs were either too dangerous or too distant.

Throughout the 1960s' the sentimental mode implied a fundamental attitude to language. Language at best was good only for getting past language. The fact that language has its own laws and imperatives, its own polity, was precisely why it was the most cunning, the most resourceful, the last enemy. And although Abbie Hoffman didn't say so, he might have said, "Shut it down to open it up." If language is a city, let it fall. Let the garden of green feeling grow—sweet like the sugar cane, wordless like the dance.

This essential sentimentality, this deep distrust of the restrictions of language, this desire to level its distinguishing features, is at the heart of why young people today cannot write, cannot shape themselves through words. And it is why so many of the cultural edifices that we raise through words are equally in disrepair.

It is this sentimental attitude, now running throughout our system, that led the editor of *English Today*, the organ of the National Council of Teachers of English, to write an article last April [1975] deriding the call from colleges for more "fundamentals" at the high school level. "The English teaching profession—for the most part—has progressed," he wrote, "well beyond thinking of writing instruction solely or principally in terms of basic skills instruction."

This is the very accent of the attitude I am describing. "Skills" is a code word for discipline, for work, for language in its particularity. The editor, a professor at Michigan State University, assures his high school clientele that that is all behind them. He would rather, judging by the titles of two suggestions for courses in his journal—"Creative Writing Without Words" and "A Visual Approach to Writing"—have students create sounds on a tape recorder, or "free-associate" from pictures, because words are dense and recalcitrant, stone that is hard to shape into statues. He would rather have students avoid meaning and grope for feeling. He would urge them not to face the reality of language, though, of course, the consequence is that they will not face or find the reality of themselves.

For that is what is at stake. That is what the neo-primitivism and sentimentality really mean—that all complexity can be avoided in the name of communality and desire. And I claim that this attitude persists because of what we are doing to language.

I believe that all of us are what we say we are— that as individuals and as a people we define through language what we have, and what we will be, and that a group of people who cannot clearly and precisely speak and write will never be a genuine society. We shape ourselves and our institutions, and we and our institutions are shaped, through those individual acts of negotiation between ourselves and our language. Without a respect for its awesome power we can never find out who we are, and thus never have to leave the child's garden of feeling and enter the city—that is, become citizens.

To deny language is finally to deny history, and that is what frightens me most about young people who cannot write, particularly those who do not know it or do not care. They have been duped. By thinking that language can be denied, in order to achieve full access to feeling, they have of course become blocked and stunted and frustrated—and at the most important level. It is a sad irony. High school and college students have been encouraged to believe that language does not require work—that if they wait they will suddenly blossom and flower in verbal mastery; that if they transcribe what they feel about anything it will somehow turn into what they think.

Clearly, to have been told all these things—and millions of school children were and are told these things—is to have been lied to. It is also to have been robbed of the only thing that everyone *does* share, the only thing that connects us each to each. Language is the medium in which the race lives; it is what we have brought from our past, and it is what has brought us from the past—our link with who we were and who we want to be.

On Behalf of the Humanities

Of all the areas in colleges and universities that will feel the assaults of inflation, the shrinking numbers of students, the devastated job market, and particularly the growing vocationalism of the young, the humanities will be hardest hit. Yet if one speaks of the values, and value, of a liberal education, the humanities ought to be central to the conversation. My concerns are for the continuing, vital existence of the humanities.

I conceive of the humanities as those areas of inquiry that are language- or better, word-centered, and I conceive of the radical humanist activity, therefore, as revolving around the interpretation of a text. My logocentricity is part of an old, relatively unphilosophical, fundamentally philological tradition. It sees language as the bearer of tradition, believes words give first principles and last things, and therefore believes that if etymology and eschatology will finally converge to clarify the life of an individual or an institution or a people, it will be because texts and the varieties of interpretation are vital concerns to that individual or institution or people. "*Connexa sunt studia humanitatis,*" said Coluccio Salutati, at the end of the fourteenth century. He was talking about the crucial role of grammar in the divine scheme of things. "Humane studies are connected to each other; religious studies are also bound each to each; it is impossible to acquire a complete knowledge of the one science without the other." If the humanist perspective sees how things secular and sacred are connected among themselves, it sees that connection through the ligatures of language. And it is the tradition of seeing from various vantage points, the principle of perspective and hence of multiple perspectives, that the humanities want to keep alive, and well.

That is my bias, which no one is obliged to share or even approve. But it is beneath what follows— which is a sense that in the last decade incoherence has often been institutionalized; that most curricula in high school and beyond are no better structured than many student papers; that where requirements were replaced by guidelines, those guidelines are so lacking in force they could not guide a vulture to week-old carrion, much less anyone to self-education. It is my sense that, in general, we still tend to apply solutions of the 1960s to problems of the 1970s and

1980s—and those solutions do not necessarily work.

The structures and the habits of mind of a period that was expansionist, federally supported and student-oriented; of a time when faith in the college or university mission as aimed at social action was at its most intense; of a time when it was easier than ever before to assert that academic work ought to be in many ways a form of social work—the specific attitudes of that period are in some places still being asserted and assumed when those days are gone. Demographic projections now point to a dramatic lessening in numbers of college-age students in the next decade. What was several years ago characterized as a continuing crisis in financing higher education will not slacken. Faculties are becoming increasingly tenure-heavy because of legislation raising retirement ages and because there are fewer new jobs. There will be—most dangerous trend of all—less need for young faculty.

The mood, indeed all the imperatives, now point to contraction, self-sufficiency, a deepening of the pressure on faculty. Those pressures come and will continue to come most insistently from two quarters: from legislative or administrative cost benefit analysis and productivity studies, and from the increasing migration of students toward more immediately "practical" and vocationally oriented subjects. Thus the humanities feel and will continue to feel this double squeeze—to justify what they do and to give others skills they can "use"—more acutely than any other segment of the university world.

It will be a hard time. While it will be true, it will not be enough to advert to the dignity of man, the connectedness among things; the way the humanities prepare for life and sharpen critical judgment, and give a keener appreciation of experience; how they express, and teach us to express, the highest values we can live by; or the way they are valuable in and of themselves. The reason this will not do is that under pressure humanists, as well as others, did not really seem to believe it. Ten to twelve years ago, it was in many places the humanists, not the hard scientists or social scientists, but the humanists, or at least people who taught in humanities departments, who wrote the guidelines that displaced the requirements for a B.A., who eloquently undermined the writing and the foreign language requirements, who instituted the grading reforms that, some would argue, did nothing to discourage other pressures that were inflating grades. You can call what happened then a new spirit of freedom; you can call it a "vocational crisis"; you can call it anything you wish. The fact remains that the humanists, self-proclaimed as central and vital links to all of experience, displaced themselves, said they were not necessary to an ordered existence, even when that existence was only undergraduate education, much less society's stream of life. And in seeming to will themselves to the periphery, humanists made themselves in subsequent hard financial times perilously vulnerable.

Early in May 1977 the faculty at a major state university in New England voted overwhelmingly for the removal of the President and the Provost, the cause for that series of votes being a plan presented by the Provost to cut a number of faculty positions and to excise two departments—Asian Studies and Slavic Languages. The language departments tend to be the first to go. The more remote, geographically, the sooner they feel the sword. When we come to European languages, it is always a nice question whether Portuguese or Italian will precede Classics when the cuts are imposed. It is an extraordinarily melancholy sight, the devastation of foreign languages in this country—the sliding enrollments and smaller and smaller numbers of faculty involuntarily justifying the analyses that proceed by the numbers. The demise of foreign languages is part of a larger assault on literacy, part of a larger decline in the capacity to handle any language at all. It is, I believe, a fact that in the last fifteen years, certainly the last ten, any American college student who knew anything about the dynamics of English—its struts and cables, its soaring spans, the way it holds together and works—knew it by analogy from the grammar of a foreign language. It is true, the old cliché, that says a foreign language necessarily deepens one's grasp of one's native language. And what is true about language tends to be true of culture. All the general worry about students' capacity to structure and to express their thoughts in English must include the current sorry situation with foreign languages.

But what do we expect? When most college faculties in this country will not require either for admission or for graduation the knowledge of a foreign language, why should hard-pressed administrations think languages are crucial? If humanities faculties do not assert the mutual dependence and reliance of the various parts, then the parts, or some parts, will disappear. No one will articulate a coherent and useful view of the humanities if the humanists will not or cannot. And if the humanists do not, then what was threatened at that university I referred to, a situation where at the end of the twentieth century a student would not be able to study Russian or Chinese, or know people who were studying them, or be able to study them in translation from people who know the original, will be more and more the norm.

These remarks on foreign languages, whose plight is visible and whose position is central to the humanities, ought to be understood as including the arts, whose plight is not so visible but whose position within the humanities is no less central. These pursuits, music, theater, painting, sculpture, architecture, each with its own sign system or "language" and its own "texts," are very much a part of my view of the humanities. Here the values we think of as humanistic are given, by a private act of the imagination, public expression and exposure. The arts are particularly vulnerable, especially in institutions without professional schools of music or art or drama or architecture to act as buffers or lobbyists. These areas are vulnerable because their faculties, either performers or practitioners, often are not seen to have

54

the clout they should have in "academic" circles; because while many students are drawn to the arts, many majors are not, aṇd the numbers are low; and most fundamentally, because the arts are still viewed in many quarters, within the academy and without, as accidental, not essential; as ornamental; as something vaguely suspect, faintly interesting and often useless, like exotic foreign languages. Again, unless humanities faculties and those sympathetic to them are willing and able to assert that the so-called creative or performing arts are as much a part of the way civilized life is ordered and given meaning as anything else is, then those pursuits may be hit and hit again. And so, eventually, will the allied faculties of musicology and the history of art, particularly at the graduate level, for the historical investigation of aesthetic objects is not especially valued where the aesthetic process has no real existence. We must not encourage such a view or appear to be unconcerned about its implications.

You may have noticed I refer in my remarks to humanities faculties, not humanities departments. Departments are often the bane as well as the prop of academic existence. We complain about them, but we regard them as indispensable. You know we have been willing to vote to abolish grades, requirements, poverty and war, but never departments. And yet I think that just as one cannot be captive, in order to survive, of attitudes of the recent past, so one cannot be captive of the administrative structures of the dimmer or dimmest past.

Departments were not brought down graven in stone. And no one wants, nor should one allow administrators, to define departments as if they were necessarily identical with areas of intellectual inquiry; or to regard areas of intellectual inquiry as if they were necessarily definable as departments. The ways people really think, teach, and especially do research are not defined solely by departments and never have been. Of course, departments are necessary for bureaucratic and organizational purposes; of course, they serve to indicate larger zones of concern and common interest, but they must be shaped and perhaps reconceived. Departments must be administered, but not as if they were sacraments.

Humanities departments must be thought of as forces in a field rather than feudal baronies. And the faculties that inhabit these departments must be willing to assert new administrative patterns, patterns that more nearly reflect the teaching and research interests of faculties and the needs and desires of undergraduate and graduate students, than the present rigid, often arbitrary boundaries do. New administrative arrangements should not be allowed to grow like toadstools after summer rain— there has to be a vital, legitimate teaching interest to justify a new cluster or association of colleagues. But I am less worried about humanities departments undergoing rapid change than I am about seeing them atrophy and, because they cannot change in a time of vocational pressure, begin to wither away. My theme is simple: academic humanists must be flexible and choose to assert themselves, even if that means consolidation of resources, even if that means changing comfortable administrative structures, before choices are forced on them, or worse, before the power to choose is denied. If humanities faculties face their responsibilities and take the lead, they will be able to change and grapple with their futures. Otherwise, hard-pressed administrations may think they must lead by invoking some principal of pseudo-equity (Everything Is as Valuable as Everything Else) and slashing across the board.

What do I mean by new administrative patterns that better reflect how things are done? Simply, to revert to an earlier example, I mean larger language departments making common cause with smaller ones, instead of viewing everyone else as competition. To the extent it is feasible, language departments might begin to explore linguistics and its insights so that some levels and kinds of language teaching might be done in common through common techniques, rather than always by each department on its own. At the very least, some training in common procedures might be given to the graduate students who do the great bulk of undergraduate language instruction everywhere.

I am talking about literature departments pooling resources—which means teaching faculties and traditions—not to teach "comparative literature" but to teach "literature." I mean the organization of faculty members and courses by definable historic periods, rather than only by languages or thematic divisions;

teaching in Classical Studies or Medieval Studies or Renaissance or Enlightenment or Modern Studies, or by cultural areas, like American or Afro-American Studies, and teaching and studying the art, history, literature, history of science, philosophy, religious thoughts of this grouping, rather than assuming each discipline or subject is forever encased in the plastic bags of the departments. We must bring together the way faculties are organized and the way they teach and think.

I am finally thinking of humanities area programs —of placing, again, a language that has or will have a hard time by itself, alone, in the context of the philosophy and history and literature and art history of that language. Organize an area that way, and suddenly languages like the Slavic ones or German or Italian, or any number of others, look very different. Strong Classics departments which teach history, philosophy, archeology, art, literature, numismatics, and papyrology as well as the Greek and Latin languages, have always been area programs. Strong Classics departments have always been those fields of force that I would like to see us at least begin to explore as models. And these models might then be better able to explore those ways of affiliating with, and thus supporting and drawing support from, the social sciences. The insights of sociology and anthropology, of political and economic thought, of psychoanalysis are part of the way we think and teach and write. Let the curriculum follow the mind, not restrain it.

I think the humanities are definable by the kinds of materials they use; I think the humanists share common interpretive modes and angles of vision; I think connections, in innumerable ways, characterize our materials and our methods. I think common values, about humane order, a decent rationality, a spacious and civilizing flexibility, inform those materials and methods. I believe the humanities bear a tradition that is a spirit as well as a collection of texts and ways of seeing.

Humanities faculties must assert themselves. They must assert those affiliations, those common connections each to each, and assert them intellectually and administratively, in theory and in practice. If those who conceive of themselves as humanists —and they are not only academic people but all who believe in a shared core of values held by educated people through language—do not speak for themselves, no one else can or will.

"Nature Justly Viewed"

Truly to be liberally educated, truly to be prepared
to meet and shape the world of this century and the
next, no man or woman can be without some grasp of
the principles of scientific inquiry, the insights of
scientific research and the various languages that
science speaks. There is a common fallacy of educational thinking that asserts that a liberal education
is synonymous with the humanities. Nothing could
be farther from the truth. A liberally educated mind
is precisely one that has composed itself sufficiently
to experience the thrill, the deeply satisfying, rous-
ing excitement, of seeing a mathematical solution
move to the same kind of inevitable, economical fulfillment of itself as does a great sonnet; one that can
derive the same pleasure from discerning and ab-

sorbing the nature of a pattern in matter as in a painting or in market behavior; that can find the same satisfaction in applying the results of technological experiments as in applying any other kind of knowledge, for the betterment of humankind. The imagination, the capacity to discover or impose a new shape with the mind, is the province of science as much as of any other form of human investigation. And the power of the imagination is finally the energy tapped and transformed by an education.

A college education can come in many settings, with many kinds of strengths. At Yale, it comes in the setting of a University College, which means that undergraduates are taught by those who also constantly and actively engage in graduate teaching and research. There is another common fallacy that asserts there is some inevitable and necessary conflict between teaching and research. Some would exalt teaching as if it could exist without research and would insist that the health of the College is separable from the University research pursuits of the faculty. I could not disagree more emphatically. Research, in whatever field, alone or in groups, done late at night or snatched at dawn, in laboratory, library or at home, pursued for a few hours a day or throughout weekends, during vacations or on leave, is the essential source from which teaching is drawn. Indeed, the strength of Yale College derives in large part from the presence of the professional schools around it and from the fact the faculty of the College is also the faculty of the Graduate

School. The needs of undergraduates are embraced by the same people who embrace their responsibilities to graduate students, to their professional disciplines, to themselves as scholars. The University is the universe in which the College exists, and the strength and coherence of the University College depends upon the collaboration of institutions and human efforts that make up the whole.

What, one might ask, does this *grand jeté* on the inseparability of teaching and research, undergraduate and graduate education, have to do with science, with what I said I was going to say? I think it has a good deal to do with it, in the following way. Science at Yale and the rise of research and graduate education at Yale followed nearly identical paths, the College giving rise to a graduate faculty that was essentially a science faculty, a science faculty that taught undergraduates and that included some of the most prominent figures American science has produced. Science at Yale came out of the heart of this place, the old brick row, just over a hundred years ago, and Yale science was at the heart of the development of professional education, and the advancement of knowledge, in America. It is a story that began in the middle of the last century, and continues powerfully today.

In 1847 the Yale Corporation established a new Department of Philosophy and the Arts, independent of Yale College, meant to embrace science and the arts; that is, "philosophy, literature, history, the moral sciences, other than law or theology, the natural sciences excepting medicine and their application to the arts." The Department was created with two professorships, of 'agricultural and of practical chemistry, and began to offer courses in 1848. The most notable part of the Department was the Yale School of Applied Chemistry, described in the College Catalogue for 1847–48 as a "Laboratory on the College grounds to provide facilities for individual study and research by students other than undergraduates." Courses in the Department were offered in chemistry, metallurgy, agricultural science and mathematics as well as in Greek, philology, Arabic and Latin, but the great preponderance of students pursued science and engineering, the number of scientists, originally six in 1847, swelling to twenty-five by 1852.

In 1852 the Corporation approved a proposal to found a School of Engineering, and in the academic year 1854–55 the Trustees combined all theoretical and applied work into the Yale Scientific School. The School, the first of its kind, included the Department of Philosophy and the Arts, and, to the existing professorships in Chemistry, Natural History, Mathematics and Physics were added new chairs in Civil Engineering, Metallurgy and Analytical Chemistry. In the meantime Mr. Joseph Sheffield was being urged by academics and townsmen alike to endow a scientific school; between 1858 and 1860 he gave handsomely of land, laboratory equipment, buildings and endowment, and in 1861 the Sheffield Scientific School was established. In

1860, the University, as it by now had every right to be called, had decided to offer a Ph.D., and thus in 1861 occurred another notable event: the first Ph.D. degrees in America were awarded by Yale, one in classics, one in philosophy, one in astronomy. In 1862, another was given in classics, and in 1863 two more in classics and one in engineering. These doctorates, particularly the first in science and engineering, grew out of the emphasis first put upon post-undergraduate research in the sciences.

Yale science continued to flourish, with another donor, George Peabody, giving "to promote the interests of Natural Science." The Peabody Museum was established in 1863; then as now one of the most distinguished centers of its kind in the country. The Peabody is one of Yale's glories, and will, I trust, continue to develop in its critical role as a center for research and instruction and collegial stimulation in the physical, biological and relevant social sciences as well as entertaining and instructing thousands of visitors annually. At the same time, from 1859 to 1871, Yale was adding chairs in Industrial Mechanics, Agriculture, Botany, Zoology, Mining, Palaeontology, Dynamical Engineering and Mathematical Physics.

During these years, another strand of scientific research that would prove so critical to the future of science and of science at Yale began to be woven into our fabric. In 1856, Samuel William Johnson was appointed Professor of Analytical Chemistry, and out of his teaching and work came the establishment of the Connecticut Agricultural Experiment Station on the Yale Campus in 1877; and from the research and teaching of his student, Russell Chittenden, came the leadership for a whole new field, known then as Physiological Chemistry, in which Chittenden took the first American Ph.D. from Yale in 1880. Chittenden had begun teaching that subject in 1874, when he was an eighteen-year-old junior in the Sheffield Scientific School, and he held the first chair in Physiological Chemistry in America in 1882. He was joined twenty years later by his student, Lafayette Mendel, and Mendel, with Thomas Burr Osborne of the Connecticut Agricultural Experiment Station, did pioneering work in protein chemistry, and on the dietary necessity of certain amino acids, and of what became known as vitamins. Here is the field of biochemistry, in the words of Professor Joseph Fruton, to whom I am indebted for this account and much more, that "area of science in which there is a conscious interplay of chemistry—the study of the properties of molecules—and biology—the study of the properties of living things." The field has had various names—"Physiological Chemistry, Biological Chemistry, Chemical Biology, Cell Physiology and, most recently, Molecular Biology" and, as Professor Fruton reminds us, "began its existence as a university discipline in the United States just about 100 years ago, and Yale was its birthplace." As the present power and distinction of Yale's Department of Molecular Biophysics and Biochemistry and the allied research in

65

the Department of Biology and the various departments of the Medical School all attest, this great tradition of leadership lives today.

The ancients believed places had geniuses who contained the spirit of a locale, and there were geniuses of the place in those days. I have alluded to some already, but two above all others deserve mention here for the science they brought to Yale, and that through them Yale took to America. The first is a towering figure, the 200th anniversary of whose birth the University celebrates this year. He is Benjamin Silliman, the person most responsible for the establishment of science and graduate education in science at Yale and for bringing the Good News of science to early nineteenth-century America. Born in Trumbull, Connecticut in 1779, he entered Yale College at thirteen, graduated in 1796, and in 1802, at the age of twenty-three, was appointed Professor of Chemistry and Natural History. Silliman had intended to be a lawyer and had completed his legal apprenticeship, but his new position seized him and, with characteristic vigor, he set about learning the subjects he would profess. He studied abroad in Philadelphia, London and Edinburgh and in 1806 believed himself prepared to teach chemistry and metallurgy full time.

Silliman served on the College faculty for fifty-one years, retiring at the age of seventy-four in 1853. He remained a force, however, until his death at eighty-five, in 1864. He oversaw the growth at Yale of chemistry, geology, metallurgy, natural history, mathematics and engineering. He also nurtured the growth of science elsewhere, for beginning when he was fifty-five he lectured throughout the land for over twenty years on geology and chemistry. In Boston, 1,500 people twice a week came to hear him lecture in the Masonic Hall for up to two hours a session. Silliman annually lectured in New York and at the new Lowell Institute near Boston, and in the next years went all over New England, the Western Reserve, to Pittsburgh, Baltimore, Charleston, Montgomery, Mobile, New Orleans, Natchez; when he was seventy-five, he lectured in St. Louis and, when he was seventy-seven, in Buffalo. He was a national figure, preaching for science in the service of God and man, an overwhelming presence, large, courtly, voluble, his lectures marked by spellbinding chemical experiments and by large drawings and specimens of rocks and fossils, his zest and oratory riveting, entertaining and instructing thousands. Silliman himself recorded the best evaluation of this teaching when he notes that he heard one man say, "He's a smart old fellow," and his neighbor reply, "Yes, he is a real steamboat."

The human imagination, through science or anything else, can either discern a design or project a new principle. Silliman was a discerner. At Pittsburgh: "True science is fitted to teach us how the laws of nature are employed to produce the happy issue which everywhere present themselves to our admiring contemplation." His was not a speculative but an admiring genius, and he gloried in the

Glory. When he was eighty-two, he wrote that in the study of science he had never forgotten to give honor to the Creator, "happy if I might be the honored interpreter of a portion of His works, and of the beautiful structure and beneficent laws discovered therein by the labors of many illustrious predecessors."

There is a moving generosity of spirit in these words as Silliman looked back at a lifetime of interpreting, through his textbooks, his lectures; through the *American Journal of Science and the Arts*, which he founded in 1818 and edited alone for twenty years; at the Department of Philosophy and the Arts, the School of Applied Chemistry, the Sheffield Scientific School; through the work of his pupils, and of his colleagues on the faculty including his son, Ben, and his son-in-law, the great naturalist, James Dwight Dana; at his work as a consulting chemist and geologist from Pennsylvania to Virginia, and at his role in organizing the American Geological Society and the American Association for the Advancement of Science. In Silliman's vision of the unity of knowledge—no separation between science and the arts; the mind of man an admiring model of the Creator's—in his reveling in the application of science to the cause and expansion of his beloved new country; as evangelist, entrepreneur, steamboat, and theologian of science, Silliman taught a nation to love the beauty and truth of what he called "nature justly viewed." And at the core of his love and belief was an educational vision that he first expressed just over one hundred and fifty years ago to the freshmen students in chemistry in Yale College, the vision of education as transcending simple utility and embracing knowledge for itself, a good from God. "It would now," he said in 1828, "be as disreputable for any person, claiming to have received a liberal education, or to possess liberal knowledge, to be ignorant of the great principles and of the leading facts of chemical as of mechanical philosophy." Courtly, shrewd, capacious Silliman—it would be hard to better that statement today and foolish to try.

And then there was another figure, who lived into our own century, also a graduate of and teacher at Yale, as different from Silliman as it was possible to be, not a discerner of design but a creator of principles, a deeply inward intellect whose clear and brooding reach, and capacity to imagine precisely and thoroughly, makes him probably the greatest American scientist ever to live. I refer to Josiah Willard Gibbs. When President Day retired, in 1846, and his house became the School of Applied Chemistry, Day returned to his family residence on Crown Street and the family then occupying the Day House, Professor of Sacred Literature Josiah Gibbs and his wife, four daughters and young son, built a home on High Street where the Berkeley Master's house now stands and where the younger Gibbs, save for three years of study in Paris, Berlin and Heidelberg, would pass his whole life. At the age of ten, in 1849, Gibbs became a student at the Hopkins Grammar School, across the street from his home, where the Law School now stands, and at fifteen enrolled in Yale College, the College of the two Sillimans, Dana, and Gibbs' mentor, Hubert Anson Newton, Professor of Mathematics. In three of his four years at Yale, Gibbs took top prizes in Latin and mathematics. After graduating in 1858, he went on to obtain in 1863 the first American Ph.D. in engineering. He was a tutor in Latin and mathematics in the College for the next three years and it is not completely fanciful, I think, to say that his gift for elegant composition in the ancient language fed his gift for compressed clarity—for elegance—in the language that is mathematics. Three years of European study in physics and mathematics built on his engineering and extended his theoretical grasp, and then Gibbs returned to Yale, to High Street, and spent his life as Professor of Mathematical Physics from 1871 until he died in 1903. He went to his office in what became Farnam, he remained a bachelor, he rarely left New Haven again save for walking vacations in northern New England or New York, and was buried in the Grove Street Cemetery, a block beyond the boyhood grammar school he served as trustee, two blocks from home.

What a modest, meticulous life, whose only outward pleasures were the picnics and suppers and outings of the Yale family, a lifelong gift for carpentry, and his science; what a contrast to Silliman, who wanted to scoop up the country in his hands and hold it up to the light. Silliman's opinions on religion, politics, science, the state of the republic were nationally known; Gibbs' are, with the rarest exceptions, impossible to discover. Silliman was imperial, a portrait of him by Samuel F. B. Morse showing a figure that dominates the natural world he is demonstrating; Gibbs was reticent without shyness or hauteur, affable, deft, never absentminded or "other-worldly" but inward, concentrated. There are, however, virtues to such interiority. When Silliman hymned the great design, his utterances often passed rapidly from a solid to a gaseous state; Gibbs' always had a terrifying pellucid density, as he sought inexorably for what he called several times the standpoint of greatest simplicity. Silliman was a geyser and a wonder to behold; Gibbs was a laser, who saw farther than anyone of his time.

Martin J. Klein, Eugene Higgins Professor of the History of Physics and the country's leading historian of physics, has remarked that Gibbs' "laconic, mathematical" style made it difficult for all but the greatest of his contemporaries to understand what he was doing. But what Gibbs was doing, particularly in his three papers published in 1873 and 1878 in the *Transactions of the Connecticut Academy of Arts and Sciences*, was to extend and complete the field of classical thermodynamics and to give a foundation for the discipline of physical chemistry.

Gibbs' greatest work, done in his thirties, built

on the theories concerning the transformation of energy into mechanical heat, developed by the German, Rudolf Clausius, and the Scotsman, William Thomson, better known as Lord Kelvin. In 1873, Gibbs had seized on the concept of entropy, which determines the energy unavailable for work in a system. He had established that the fundamental thermodynamic equation for a system expressed its energy in terms of its entropy and volume, and from that essential insight flowed much of Gibbs' greatest work in 1878 on the nature of equilibrium, work that, in the words of Professor Klein, "vastly extended the domain covered by thermodynamics, including chemical, elastic, surface, electromagnetic and electrochemical phenomena in a single system." His vision was boundless.

This massive and continuous act of the imagination, combining physics, mathematics and chemistry, by a virtual unknown, in a small town in Connecticut, published in a journal of exceedingly limited circulation, came gradually to be recognized for the overwhelming achievement it was, and by the time its creator had published, at the end of his life, his great study of statistical mechanics, he was recognized for the genius that he was. Throughout it all, Gibbs had never wavered as a scientist or man from the principle he expressed with characteristic conciseness in a letter to the American Academy of Arts and Sciences in 1881 accepting its prestigious Rumford Medal: "One of the principal objects of theoretical research in any department of knowledge is to find the point of view from which the subject appears in its greatest simplicity." His students loved the man as deeply as they were shaped by his work, and Gibbs' impact, as a scientist and human being, continued at Yale in the career of Nobel Laureate Lars Onsager, who held the Gibbs Professorship, and continues through the present incumbent of that chair, Fëza Gursey.

How great a scientist was Gibbs? My capacities are exhausted by asking the question. But I can report the answer implicit in the comment of one supremely qualified to judge. At the end of his life, Albert Einstein was interviewed by the Canadian scientist A. V. Douglas. "There remained," writes Douglas, "one special thing I wanted to ask him. Who were the greatest men, the most powerful thinkers whom he had known? The answer came back without hesitation, 'Lorentz.' . . . 'But,' he added. 'I never met Willard Gibbs; perhaps had I done so, I might have placed him beside Lorentz.' "

Gibbs, Silliman and the others belong to all of science, theoretical and applied, and to its ongoing life, and I hope that my amateur's account does not carry a tone excessively parochial, for parochialism would more than anything contravene the spirit and substance of their achievements as scientists. And yet we at Yale should take a justifiable pride in the contributions these scientists have made, and their successors continue to make, to this place and to the country; we should not be cautious about celebrating them and what they stood for, or in finding satisfaction that they and their latter-day colleagues nourish, with so many others, the educational aspirations of our University.

And let us remember that those scholars who worked so hard to found the scientific school and the Ph.D., who established Yale, through science and other subjects, as a University, also taught in a College, many remaining on its faculty, all encouraging the younger students. That fluidity of passage by faculty between undergraduate and graduate teaching, between research and formal instruction; that accessibility, that concern for the community of ideas and healthy disregard of boundaries— where they only impede the pursuit of learning—is what comes through most clearly in the rise of science and graduate research at Yale. And that spirit, that turned a College into a University, and forged the University College of a particular kind, that spirit of collaboration among people and ideas, continues to be the hallmark of this place, and is one of the many gifts the science faculties of Yale bring to the insitution. For this historical outline is really the outline of a continuing tradition here; you will find some of the most innovative teaching at Yale among the scientists, and among those most distinguished nationally for research in science often the clearest sense of the educational needs of the young student. This spirit shaped by scientists over a century ago retains its force today.

From the scientists, social and natural, we derive our belief in the unifying force of the search for knowledge, and in the harmonies among forms of knowledge, even as knowledge, increasing, tends to fragment itself and us with it. From them we learn what we should never forget, that to view nature justly, nature human and material, we must eschew parochialism and casual labels and bureaucratic boundaries, and seek to see the truth from as many vantage points as humankind can summon. That search for ways of seeing the truth humanely and wholly is the role of a great university.

NOTE: I have drawn heavily on various sources in this essay, and none must be blamed for whatever vagaries of interpretation or errors are contained herein. For the rise of science in graduate education I have relied on Edgar S. Furniss, *The Graduate School at Yale: A Brief History* (New Haven: 1965), and for these matters and Silliman, on *Benjamin Silliman and His Circle: Studies on the Influence of Benjamin Silliman on Science in America*, edited by Leonard G. Wilson (New York: Science History Publications, 1979), particularly the essays of Wilson, John C. Greene and Louis I. Kuslan. The citations from Silliman, Sr. are drawn from Greene's essay. For Gibbs, I have used the basic biography by Lynde Phelps Wheeler, *Josiah Willard Gibbs. The History of a Great Mind* (New Haven and London: Yale University Press, 1952), and, most of all, have drawn heavily on the goodwill and scholarship of Professor Martin J. Klein, particularly his essay, "Gibbs on Clausius" in Russell McCormmach, ed. *Historical Studies in the Physical Sciences*, I (Philadelphia: 1969), pp. 127–49; his contribution on Gibbs to the *Dictionary of Scientific Biography* (New York: 1972), 5:386–93, and his "The Early Papers of J. Willard Gibbs: A Transformation of Thermodynamics," a paper presented at the XVth International Congress of the History of Science (1977), now published in revised form in *Human Implications of Scientific Advance*, ed. E. G. Forbes (Edinburgh: Edinburgh University Press, 1978). Professor Klein also kindly provided me with the passage from the Douglas interview with Einstein, "Forty Minutes with Einstein," *Journal of the Royal Astronomical Society of Canada*, 50 (1956), p. 99. I am also indebted to Joseph S. Fruton, Eugene Higgins Professor of Biochemistry, for allowing me to use material from his unpublished paper on the history of biochemistry at Yale, presented to the Department of Molecular Biophysics and Biochemistry, April 9, 1979.

Yale and Athletics

As is customary, we can discover how we think about ourselves by looking at how we speak about ourselves. Two words of ancient Greek, *athlōn* and *athlōs*, shape a third, *athletēs*. *Athlōs* meant a contest; *athlōn*, a prize won in a contest, and they provide us with *athletēs*, an individual competing for a prize in the public games. Here in small compass is much of the ancient Greek world. Life and all that is valuable is seen as a contest. Struggle and contention lie at the core of everything, and one must devote all one's being to winning. If one wins, there is a prize, a tangible mark of triumph in the endless competition. Merit, skill, capacity—call it what you will—must be tested, and if victorious, rewarded.

No part of Greek life was immune to this view of competition or to the possibility of triumph. If you won a footrace or a chariot race, you could ask Pindar to immortalize your achievement in an ode; if you were Aeschylus or Sophocles or Euripedes, and you won the annual three-day contest for dramatists in Athens, you gained a prize. By the fifth century B.C., what we would call the realms of the athletic and the artistic were not separate in the intensity of competition or in the assumption that reward would follow victory or in the importance placed on the activities by the culture. The athlete and the artist lived in the same world and did the same thing: they both asserted the spirit in order to thrust the individual beyond time and achieve something permanent.

A sense of proportion between the exertions of body and mind was essential to the shaping of a triumph or a life, and this perspective is concisely expressed in the dialogue between Socrates and Glaucon in the third book of Plato's *Republic*. Socrates sums it up:

> . . . it seems there are two arts which I would say some god gave to mankind, music and gymnastics, for the service of the high-spirited and the love of knowledge in them—not for the soul and body incidentally, but for the harmonious adjustment of these two principles by the proper degree of tension and relaxation of each. (412)

An earlier, Homeric ethos of winning at any cost was transmuted by Plato's time into a strict observance of the rules and a deep sense that the law was essential to survival. The toughness, however, of their ancestors remained part of the Greek soul that Plato was so concerned to reform; for while Plato asserted physical training and games as explorations of knowledge of the spirit on behalf of a healthy citizen and healthy state, he never considered athletics as pleasurable in itself. Nor did he have any idea of sportsmanship, or of what we call character building. In Plato, physical training and games are part of the necessary regimen that will make a soul shapely and balanced and thus defend it against impurities, and defend a city against its enemies. The concept of athletics as important for creating other values, of teamwork, moral character, social equity, comes as a legacy from nineteenth-century England.

The English before the nineteenth century enjoyed sport—some bloody, some not, but in most cases unorganized. Only somewhat over a century ago, in the 1850s and 1860s, were the rules of many games codified, with the rules of Rugby football having been set in 1846. That game carries the name of a great English public school, and indeed the reform of that school, under Dr. Thomas Arnold, and of the other old public schools, is central to the history of the rise of organized games in England. In those schools, and the ones founded at mid-century on their model, games began to assume overwhelming importance. The sage and serious Dr. Arnold and his epigones were intent, through their sermons and their schools, on training Christian gentlemen for service to Church and State and sport was not, at least to Arnold, an important ingredient in the moral recipe for a responsible Christian servant of society. But Arnold's notion of his school was not the notion the world enjoyed. In 1858, a former student of Arnold's, Thomas Hughes, wrote an immensely successful and influential novel about a boy at Rugby. The novel was called *Tom Brown's School Days*, and it presented another Rugby, the Rugby where games were the heart of school life and of the making of a brother in what came to be called the fellowship of muscular Christians.

A Master in *Tom Brown's School Days* says of cricket that the "discipline and reliance on one another, which it teaches, are so valuable." In an educational philosophy where character is more important than intellect and teamwork more valued than individuality, games are the teachers; the school is simply the place where the games happen. By mid-century, as Asa Briggs has said, games are "institutions," and on the fields of those institutions develop ideals of sportsmanship, and fair play, and team spirit, and the development of character for later life, which are still with us. How different are those from the Greek ideals. The Greeks saw physical training and games as a form of knowledge, meant to toughen the body in order to temper the soul; activities pure in themselves, immediate, obedient to the rules so that winning would be sweeter still. The English ideals, on the other hand, aim beyond the field to the battleground of life, and they emphasize fellowship, sacrifice, a sense that how one plays is an emblem of how one will later behave; they teach that victory is ultimately less important than the common experience of struggling in common. Discipline and a view of life as a contest are part of both attitudes, but the two concepts of the value and purpose of athletics are as different as they can be, as different as exalting a shining, individual winner, and cherishing a character that effaces itself in the team.

We inherit these distinct views of athletics, each with its own aspects of cult, each placing athletics within an educational framework, each devoted to an amateur ideal. Both views are held in common by individuals and by institutions to this day, but they coexist uneasily. That ambivalence exists within our own Ivy Group—those institutions most closely modeled on the English public schools and universities, where organized collegiate competition grew up in America in the nineteenth century— and that ambivalence is easily stated: does one place the highest value on winning or does one subordinate victory to the larger values of an educational institution? We think we have chosen the latter idea, but we are nervous, nervous because we do not want to lose at anything, any more than Tom Brown, or Frank Merriwell, did. The ambivalence about how to merge winning and education is writ large in the country's ambivalence about big-time

81

collegiate athletics. It was obvious in the national debate about the 1980 Summer Olympics—the Greeks among us, believing in their individual destinies, wanted to go to Moscow and win; the Celts among us, team members all, played along with President Carter.

Where does Yale stand in 1980? Do organized games and physical training have any role in our modern University, and if they do, what are their purposes? If my sketch of how athletics has come to us is valid, it is clear that we behave like the English and think like the Greeks. But to create a contest between the ancients and the moderns and then to stand as spectators at the match trying to decide which side to root for is not enough. We must know if athletics figures in our educational scheme, and if so, how. I believe that athletics is part of an education of a young person, as the Greeks and the English schoolmasters believed: and I believe athletics is part of an education because athletics teaches lessons valuable to the individual by stretching the human spirit in ways that nothing else can. Is there a view of education that will contain this conviction concerning athletics?

There is, and I can offer it in no better way than by citing one of the subtlest and most powerful minds of the nineteenth century, another Englishman who thought profoundly about the nature of education. I refer to John Henry Cardinal Newman and *The Idea of a University*. In the fifth discourse of that work, Cardinal Newman distinguishes "liberal" education from "servile" or useful education. ". . . there are bodily exercises," he says, "which are liberal, and mental exercises which are not so."* Those pursuits that are intellectual and not liberal are those of a professional or commercial education. He then turns to exercises of the body which are, in his sense, liberal.

> Such, for instance, was the palaestra, in ancient times; such the Olympic games, in which strength and dexterity of body as well as of mind gained the prize. In Xenophon we read of the young Persian nobility being taught to ride on horseback and to speak the truth; both being among the accomplishments of a gentleman.

And what is the conceptual grounding that allows for this view of physical training as "liberal"? ". . . that alone is liberal knowledge," says Newman, "which stands on its own pretensions, which is independent of sequel, expects no complement, refuses to be *informed* (as it is called) by any end, or absorbed into any art, in order duly to present itself to our contemplation. The most ordinary pursuits have this specific character, if they are self-sufficient and complete; the highest lose it, when they minister to something beyond them."

Newman drew upon Aristotle and other Greek thinkers to go beyond them, and to develop a view

* Citations throughout are from the 1968 edition of Holt, Rinehart and Winston, New York.

of a liberal education that also had his own culture's stamp upon it. We recognize that stamp when he says that education is higher than instruction because education "implies an action upon our mental nature, and the formation of a character. . . ." Various philosophies of education, therefore, come together in Newman's idea of a liberal education, and various notions of athletics cluster too, in the larger vision here projected so powerfully. It is a vision to inspire us still, where the discrete character of the pursuit, physical or mental, is the essence; where the lack of expectation of sequel, the absence of an end except the enactment of the pursuit itself, makes the pursuit a liberal one. Thus an athletic contest construed as enjoyable in itself, with no expectation of a consequence beyond the playing of it, as hard and as fully as possible, is a natural and inevitable part of a program of education called, in Newman's (and my) terms, "liberal."

Such an ideal of education, and of the proper place of athletics within it, should be with us to this day, in this place, and must shape our thinking. Such a liberal education, properly understood, supports athletics as an essential part of the educational process. It is equally consistent with this view, however, that athletics not outstrip that larger process, or deviate from it. Such an ideal means that we no more encourage a professionalism of spirit in athletics in our undergraduates than we encourage a professional view of the purpose of an undergraduate education. It means we believe in an education that is a process of exploration and fulfillment, not a process of pursuing a career.

Consistent with this perspective is Plato's idea of the necessity for proportion in things of the spirit. And thus we must remember that it is our obligation to consider our students as students above all else, and to treat them in an evenhanded fashion, and to construct their athletic programs so that their time to develop as thinking and feeling human beings is not deformed by the demands of athletic pursuits. The time and effort given to athletics by a student must be proportioned in such a way that the student has more time and energy for studies than for sports. Yale is not the place for Tom Brown; his Rugby and Oxford had their still air broken often by the cries of players but never by the rustling of a page. There must be at Yale, in philosophy and in actuality, proportion in how the institution shapes itself and in how it encourages and sanctions a student's behavior. Athletics is essential but not primary. It contributes to the point, but it is not the point itself.

By "athletics" in what follows, I mean formal sports systematically pursued, physical training and physical recreation. In thinking about athletics this way, one realizes immediately that many more people than students are involved. And therefore while it is appropriate to have a view of athletics within education for undergraduates, and we do, we must also remember that there are an equal number of graduate and professional students at Yale. For many of them, various forms of athletics are important. Within the University community there are also postdoctoral students, staff, faculty, alumni, and the spouses of all these people, for whom access to and use of activities and facilities are important. Athletics generously conceived, therefore, touches thousands throughout the Yale community. When we construct principles according to which the University will allocate its resources for athletics, we must place an educational vision at the core, but we must also remember that it is a community of people larger than any student body. In constructing principles, we must remember also that Yale's physical facilities for athletics need their share of resources, else a distinguished physical asset will continue to deteriorate and a whole community will be impoverished. Finally, we need always to recall that the production of revenue is as much a part of the picture of Yale athletics as the provision of services and opportunities. Yet as we seek actively to increase revenue so that growing expenses can be borne, we must be extraordinarily careful. We cannot increase revenues by exploiting students simply as athletes, or by allowing others to displace the Yale community for whom the physical resources are first intended. Most important, we cannot do anything to increase revenue that would in any way impair the general educational mission of the University. The management of all these ideas, and of the people, places and human efforts they involve, is a complex and fascinating task, and Yale is extremely fortunate to have a Director of Athletics, Physical Education and Recreation, Frank Ryan, who is also a member of the faculty, a lecturer in the Department of Mathematics. He embodies an understanding of the University's teaching and scholarly mission. In the Director, the University's commitment to athletics as part of the larger nature and purpose of the University is made manifest.

That commitment also informs the following principles that guide and will guide the University as it thinks of athletics and as it allocates scarce resources to athletics.

The first principle, already implicitly set forth, is that there must be a broadly based program of athletic opportunities, of a competitive and non-competitive sort, on a variety of levels.

The key phrase is broadly based, because this is a total community. To indicate the extent to which some form of athletic activity is important to Yale, let me offer some statistics. Despite the fact that Yale does not offer courses for credit in physical education, and no longer has a physical education requirement for graduation, this year some 9,000 individuals have used the Payne Whitney Gymnasium on some basis. Not quite half were undergraduates, including 77 percent of the men and 80 percent of the women enrolled in Yale College; the others were about 3,000 graduate and professional students and some 2,000 faculty, staff and others and their families. Not all the users paid a fee because not all asked for a direct service, but that many people, and probably more, used Payne Whitney at some point.

When one thinks of how many used the gymnasium often, it is an extraordinary amount of activity.

For a fee, there was this year even more activity. In the fall term, people took classes in aquatics, martial arts, exercise, dance and a wide variety of sports, taught by instructors in physical education and by varsity coaches. The total number here was over 2,000; most were students at all levels in the University. Thus thousands used Yale facilities, indoor and outdoor, with and without the benefit of coaching or instruction. I believe we must sustain this broad program that allows for formal and informal physical activity, by individuals and by groups, at all seasons, for all purposes. America needs citizens who know how to cherish fitness of the body along with fitness of the mind.

The second principle, focused on Yale College, follows from the first and it is that the intramural program for athletics within the residential college system must be nourished and sustained. The residential colleges are essential to an education in Yale College. They are far more than simply residences because of the energy of the academic, literary, musical, theatrical, social and athletic life contained within them, and they provide intelligible, manageable communities for advising, teaching, learning, and life. The intramural competition among the colleges is a critical element in the system's success. Again, statistics reveal part of the story. Of the roughly 10,500 applicants to the class of 1983, 6,900, or 66 percent, noted on their applications participation at the varsity level in secondary school. Such a figure indicates an extraordinarily high degree of interest and involvement in athletics on the part of many young people, and it accounts for the high levels of participation in intramural sports. Last year, some 4,800 engaged in intercollege athletics during the fall, winter and spring seasons; this year, some 3,600 played during the fall and winter. Even assuming that some students participate in more than one season, the numbers engaged in this form of residential college life are impressive and confirm my conviction that the intramural program is essential to the health of the colleges and, therefore, to the vitality of the undergraduate educational experience.

My third principle speaks to a specific type of athletic activity: we must encourage a group of varsity sports that aspire to high intercollegiate achievement within the context of the Ivy Group. Yale currently [1980] has 37 varsity sports* squads, the largest number offered by an institution in the Ivy Group. In this area, we must strive to do what we do well, by providing coaching, which is to say, teaching, of the highest quality, facilities and equipment adequate to the needs and talents of the students involved, and an atmosphere of aspiration to excellence within the spirit of a liberal education and the context of the Ivy Agreement of 1954.

Varsity sports are important, though not more important than intramural athletics or the broad pro-

* Now, 33 in 1981.

gram of opportunities offered the whole community. We must recognize that varsity athletics is the most expensive part of the total athletic program, and we must find appropriate ways to increase the revenue flowing from varsity sports. We must also recognize that it will doubtless be necessary to do fewer things, in this area of Yale as in others, in order to do what we do as well as possible.

In thinking about varsity athletics, we must understand that coaching is crucial and that the highest standard of coaching must be sought here as it must be sought in all other programs of a teaching nature in the University. Budgetary realities will mean that coaches will have to teach in the future in more than one area, whether those areas are two varsity sports, as happens now in soccer and tennis, or are in the areas of a varsity sport and physical education. I believe it must be widely acknowledged as well that recruiting is not coaching, and that the present practice of the recruitment of students who are athletes cannot encroach upon the time and effort that must be devoted to working with the students who are here, working with them and teaching them in one form or the other. I will return to this point later.

We all know that varsity athletics is the most visible part of the athletics program. It is the one some alumni, and others, find most immediately available as a form of connection with Yale. When a program in History or Physics or Divinity or Nursing is lessened or dropped, the people who think

90

most fondly of Yale in terms of the Departments of History or Physics, or the Schools of Divinity or Nursing, do not feel as immediately betrayed as alumni and others seem to when the same process of necessary, and carefully considered, reduction goes on among varsity sports. In short, pressure groups flare up quickest in this area. And yet, if we insist, as I do, that athletics is essential to the larger educational program and purposes of Yale, then athletics at all levels cannot expect to be immune to the pressures afflicting all the other parts of the University. With regard to varsity athletics, some changes will continue to be made so that we can afford to do what we will do at the level of excellence Yale must expect.

Considerable numbers of students are involved in varsity sports—by no means as many as the people who use Payne Whitney Gymnasium and its resources or as many as the students who exploit the athletic possibilities in the residential colleges, but a good number nevertheless. In 1979, 1,264 students, or 20 percent of the undergraduate body, participated at the varsity level in three seasons. In some important ways, those varsity programs are in very good condition. We have done more, for instance, as a University than almost any institution in America on behalf of women's sports at the varsity level, and the record of Yale women in all-Ivy competition is good. As a percentage of wins to contests, the record of our women varsity athletes has declined from a high of .808 in 1976–77 to an all-Ivy percentage of wins through the fall and winter seasons of this year of .571. That decline indicates an increase in competitiveness in the Ivy Group, not a diminishment of commitment to excellence at Yale. The others are catching up. The situation with regard to winning percentages in the area of men's varsity athletics is improving. In 1976–77, the men's percentage of wins to contests in the Ivy Group was .378; through the fall and winter seasons of this year it is .525. Why do I cite these percentages? Why do I bring up the won-lost records in assessing the health of varsity athletics? Because I want there to be no doubt about what I believe. I think winning is important. Winning has a joy and discrete purity to it that cannot be replaced by anything else. Winning is important to any man's or woman's sense of satisfaction and well-being. Winning is not everything but it is something powerful, indeed beautiful, in itself, something as necessary to the strong spirit as striving is necessary to the healthy character. Let all of us without bashfulness assert what the Greeks would find it absurd to suppress. Having said that, and meaning it, I repeat what I said above: our commitment to excellence, of aspiration and achievement, is based on the basic presupposition that athletics plays a properly proportioned role within our educational philosophy and program.

There are ways, however, in which our varsity, and other, sports activities are not well-off. Our facilities are not in good shape; some of them are in very poor shape. Within the context of the total University need to do maintenance, renovation and refurbishment, we must improve these athletic facilities. They are at the disposal of thousands of people and are an integral part of the quality of the University. We must be first-rate in all things, and if we will not tolerate second-rate laboratories or libraries or faculty or students, we cannot tolerate mediocrity here. Next fall we will announce an effort to raise money for athletic facilities, and for other parts of the University's total program as well.

Our fourth principle in making athletic decisions is that there must be opportunities for instruction and competition in a wide variety of physical skills. I have referred already to our programs and resources in physical education and to our commitment to individual recreation. There are others. We may well find that some varsity sports can only be sustained at a sub-Ivy level of competition, with part-time coaching or schedules that do not involve great amounts of travel. We ought also to remember that Yale fields eighteen club sports, ranging from badminton through frisbee to women's rugby. Club sports are the result of student initiative; the Department of Athletics, Physical Education and Recreation provides no administrative or technical support—that is, it does not schedule contests or provide coaches—but it does offer modest funding for equipment and travel. This year, 360 people participated in club sports, and now that the applications for club status from women's rugby and men's and women's polo are approved, the number will be larger. The club program is inexpensive; it is important as a way of providing an outlet for genuine interest without an elaborate administrative superstructure. Newman's ideal of the self-contained liberal pursuit fits the club activities elegantly.

We now come to the mode of administration of athletics at Yale. In the largest sense, Yale athletics is governed by the educational principles and mission of the University; specifically, Yale athletics is governed by the agreements set down in the Ivy Agreement of 1954 and its subsequent refinements. The letter and spirit of these agreements are central to Yale's ongoing view of athletics, and I will return to this point later.

Internally, the responsibility for and authority over athletic matters in terms of policy and procedures are delegated to the Director of the Department of Athletics, Physical Education and Recreation. The Director is appointed by the Yale Corporation upon the recommendation of the President, and the Director shapes matters of policy with the President. At the President's request, the Director also reports to the Corporation on athletic matters. For budgetary matters, the Director is responsible to the Provost and the University Budget Committee. Within this framework, the Director is in full charge of the Department and its policies and personnel. There are other groups interested in athletics, such as the AYA Committee on Athletics, which comes from this body and reports to the alumni, the University Council Committee on Athletics, which advises the President, and the seventeen Alumni Sports Associations, which assist in raising money for various teams. None of these groups, however, welcome and useful as they are, has any direct role in the management of athletics at Yale.

The Director consults with groups internal to the University. There is a Students' Users Committee, a group that meets upon its own call with the Director and that is composed of five undergraduates, appointed by the Yale College Council, and three graduate or professional students, appointed by the Graduate-Professional Student Senate. There is another student group, one that the Director has taken the initiative in forming and which he consults, in this case composed of the captains of the various varsity squads. And there is a third group, perhaps the most involved of all, a body growing out of the old Board of Athletic Control and then revised by the Jones Commission Report of 1976 and called the Athletic Executive Committee. Since its revision in 1976, this committee of faculty and administrators has never in fact functioned in an executive fashion and it could not. It should, however, be an advisory group to the Director, and I propose now to clarify that committee's function and to present it with a name and a charge appropriate to its character and duties. The purpose of this new committee, whose composition is not significantly different from that suggested by the Jones Commission Report, is to bring the advice of the faculty into the management structure of athletics at Yale in such a way that the central academic values of the University are present in the formation and review of athletic policy and procedure. Our conviction that athletics has an appropriate and essential role to play in the educational process is best given life by involving knowledgeable, experienced faculty in a collegial relationship with the Director.

The name of the committee will be the Faculty Committee on Athletics. Its membership will consist of six members of the Yale faculty, to include one residential college Master and one member of a professional school faculty. The term of service will be three years, with two members rotating off after each year. In addition, there will be an associate dean of Yale College, *ex officio*. The members of the Committee will be appointed by the President to advise the Director, who will be chairman of the Committee.

The charge to the Committee is simply stated and important:

(1) to provide advice and consultation on issues brought to its attention by the Director;

(2) to bring forward for the Director's consideration any area of concern or interest which pertains to athletic policy;

(3) to review and scrutinize Yale's athletic policy;

(4) to consult with the Director on matters

of appointments and terminations and to confirm that appropriate procedures have been followed in actions resulting in either appointment or termination;

(5) to provide a responsible voice to the Yale community regarding the course of Yale athletics;

(6) to provide annually to the President and the Officers a report on the status of athletics at Yale, with particular regard to the relation of athletics to the academic purposes of the institution.

In a very real sense, this Committee and its charge speak to the heart of the concern expressed by the Jones Commission Report, which was: does Yale really care about athletics? The answer is unequivocally yes, Yale did care and will care; Yale cares enough to assert that athletics plays a vital part in the education of its young people and in the ongoing life of everyone else. As a sign of its commitment to athletics, Yale will treat athletics according to the same central educational values and with the same desire for excellence that it brings to its other essential parts.

After this look at our educational philosophy, at the principles and priorities established for athletics, and at the means by which these convictions will be translated into action within the University, where are we? We are ready for the future. And the future, while it will build on our strengths, also presents us with problems. We know about the problems with our athletic facilities. I will only repeat what I have said: if we are to attract people of the highest quality to Yale, for athletics and for other pursuits, then we must have facilities of the highest quality. That statement is particular to athletics and general to the whole University.

I believe, however, that we have problems of another sort as well, problems with regard to the Ivy Agreement of 1954. While every Ivy institution observes the financial aid policies set forth in that agreement, there are other areas where we have drifted away from the original statement. Because I believe this to be the case, and because I believe Yale should be in the lead in reaffirming the spirit and intent of the basic Ivy Agreement, I brought to my fellow presidents in the Ivy Group in December 1979 a set of proposals and positions designed to bring us back to the basic principles. These proposals, now being studied by the Policy Committee of the Ivy Group, represent four areas where I intend to press as hard as I can for revision and reform. In these areas, I believe there is a lack of proportion, an imbalance, in the way the programs in athletics in the Ivy Group have been allowed to grow. The result of this disproportion is, in my opinion, that some students, and not a trivial number, spend far, far too much time, with the encouragement of the institutions, on athletic pursuits;

the result is that coaching has gone a long, long way, particularly in some sports, to being a matter of recruiting and not of teaching; the result is that athletics in the Ivy Group now hungers for that next event, that sequel, that bigger-league look and feel, that I think violates the essence of what we believe the role of organized athletics in our institutions ought to be. If the Ivy Group wants to be more than a set of financial aid policies and a concatenation of schedules, then I think it must return to its first principles. Else, as a group and as individual institutions, we will lose precisely what is liberating and fulfilling in our kind of college athletics and we will gain nothing save the scorn of those who wonder why we act in a fashion so inconsistent with our ideals and principles.

The proposals I made to my colleagues are the following:

We must, as a Group, discuss restricting recruiting by coaches to on-campus conversations and visits. It is, in my judgment, wrong to spend more for off-campus recruiting of students who are also athletes than is spent on the recruitment of students in general. Nor is it acceptable to the spirit of my proposal to designate an officer in the central admissions office as having a special, full-time responsibility for the recruitment of athletes. We all must recruit students for our institutions nationally, but I do not believe we should send our coaches to recruit students who are athletes as a special group. The present practices now pursued in varying ways everywhere only tend to create separate groups of students; these practices only escalate the competition for stars; they only force more and more of coaching to become hustling in the hustings. As I have said, coaching is teaching—valuable, honorable and difficult. I believe it is demeaning to the profession of coaching when one has to spend so much time traveling and wooing off-campus.

We must, as a Group, cease to think of post-season competition in any varsity sport as the natural or even necessary consequence of victory. The Ivy Group championship must be the goal of our students, and where the Ivy championship is not the major goal, or is a figment only of the daily press' imagination, then the status of Ivy championships must be elevated and affirmed. What I find so injurious to our principles and to the education of our students is the pressure to prepare for the next step, the amount of time and effort expended to get ready for what follows the regular season, the insidious sense that there is nothing valuable in the experience of being first-rate within your own league and that one has to complete some sequence to the national level. I am frankly not impressed with the argument that says: why can't we be excellent (or, you say we should be excellent) and therefore why can't we test ourselves against the best? Yale students are among the best; they are tested, and will be tested, with the best all their lives. It is to misconceive a Yale education, however, to think that education is intended simply to be the setting for a national-level athletic career in anything. If athletic gifts are there, and they blossom after graduation, fine. But Yale is not the place to come if the purpose of coming is to spend disproportionate amounts of time on athletics in order to compete beyond the Ivy Group while in college. I genuinely believe in Newman's ideal of a liberal education, an education designed at its heart not for what comes next but for the fulfillment of the pursuit, and the person, in and of itself. The spirit of post-season competition, in my view, violates that principle, whether that principle is construed as general to education or as specific to athletics.

We must, as a Group, reexamine our schedules of practice and of play in athletics, in terms of both their length and their scope. In the Ivy Group I think we have in general regulated football well, and I say that knowing that I think ten games to a season is one too many and that a pre-season scrimmage, adding in effect one more game, should not be allowed. I cannot, however, express the same confidence at all with regard to other sports, like hockey and basketball. In those, and others, we play at the varsity level seasons that I think are too long and schedules that move way beyond the Ivy Group into a staging area for national competition. Needless to say, I find such situations consistent with neither our educational principles nor our students' educational needs. I believe a number of

101

sports need examination in terms of their schedules of practice and play at the highest level of the Ivy Group.

We must, as individual institutions, if not as a Group, explore seriously the practice of multi-seasonal coaching assignments, that is, of requiring coaches to span more than one athletic season. If I am told that a given season begins too early or ends too late to allow such an arrangement, then my reply is that the season is probably too long; if I am told that a coach may have obligations with his players after the normal end of a season, then my reply is that we should not allow post-season competition; and if I am told that travel occupies, necessarily, a great deal of a coach's time after the season, then my reply is that we should not require, or allow, off-campus recruiting by coaches. My point is that coaches *are* teachers, and that they must not be made into something else by the multiple pressures brought about by present recruitment practices, post-season opportunities, and swollen schedules. A gifted coach, and there are many, can and ought to work with students in various contexts. Members of the faculty do; it is part of the pleasure, part of the job, part of the profession.

My first three proposals in particular are areas where I believe the Ivy institutions must act in concert. They need to act together for two reasons: it is impossible for one institution to act unilaterally and still remain in the Group in any realistic or practical sense; and these institutions, having agreed

to place athletics within similar educational programs, governed by a similar philosophy, must act
in concert if they wish to affirm the integrity not
only of their athletic activities but also of their larger
programs and of that liberal philosophy.

Within an overall philosophy of education, the
Ivy Group wants to combine, in athletics, training of
skills and character with a joy in winning. I believe
all the Ivy institutions want this and I believe it is a
right and proper thing to want. I am convinced that
if we go back to the first principles and to the spirit
of our Agreement, we will find again, through common effort, a structure for the educational values,
the sense of proportion in athletics and the sheer
pleasure in hard competition among ourselves that
we all want, and none of us wants to lose.

For my part, I commit Yale toward that end. It is
a goal consistent with our belief in athletics as important to the educational program of our students
and to the healthy life of our whole community. It
is a goal consistent with our deepest conviction concerning a liberal education and a necessary proportion in a civilized, fruitful life. There is a strong
spirit at Yale, a strong spirit compounded of respect
for the glories of mind and body striving in harmony; and let there be no doubt about what we have
affirmed or any doubt about what we have projected.
The educational ideals and principles that I have
asserted must *be* Yale's athletic policy; they must be
as a seamless garment, for it is our students and
their education that are finally at issue. It is our stu-

103

dents for whom our principles and beliefs are intended; it is our students who deserve a place with purpose and proportion. It is our students in whom the spirit that is Yale will live, and it is they who most deserve to know upon what ground of belief we stand, and why we have chosen to stand there.

Private Sector, Public Control and the Independent University

In a private university, we hear constantly from well-wishers and others that the private character of a private university will be lost if we do not beware the federal government and its regulatory tentacles. The private universities and their faculties need little warning. They know that something irreplaceable is lost in relying only on a centralized bureaucracy and its various arms for sustenance or guidance. They know traditions of self-reliance and of self-government, in institutions as in individuals, must be safeguarded. And I assume everyone knows that federal regulation can often be disruptive, or diversionary of resources and energy, or at times blatantly intrusive into the heart of the academic enterprise.

Beginning about a century ago, with the railroads, the federal regulatory process intended to bring equity of treatment into the commercial world. Since then, the intention of regulation by the government has been to overcome obstacles set up by those intent on monopolizing the marketplace or on ignoring the legitimate claims to social goods of the citizenry at large. The intention of regulation, to promote access and equity, cannot be quarreled with. But the effects of much regulation over the last hundred years cannot be regarded with anything but skepticism by those concerned with the Republic. Intent on promoting deeply desirable ends, the regulatory system has often effectively prevented that which it was meant to insure. The process has often become an instance of what it was intended to overcome. The regulatory solvent meant to unblock impediments to the free flow of social goods and commercial efforts has sometimes become not a solvent at all, but a spreading mucilage, self-creating, self-fulfilling, and at worst self-defeating— promoting a potential but unrealized social or commercial benefit often without any discernible regard for the costs or for the potential social injury that may, from another point of view, result; often expressing benign and desirable intent with no awareness at all of the complex, grainy, recalcitrant reality that makes up daily life. The regulatory process distrusts the imagination; the result is that federal regulations represent a threat to the imaginative capacities of the American people second only to daytime television.

The authors of regulations are hard to find. Regulations are created by committees; few are willing to take responsibility for a given spool of federal piety. Legislative histories in the Congress are often unclear, offering only the broad mandate to eradicate all harm. It is usually left to some agency or department to specify the will of the people, an act carried out under the miasma generated by the hot breath of remorseless lobbyists, who have been instructed to disagree or co-opt. I have heard congressmen, who were instrumental in passing a given federal bill, debate how best to subvert its effects now that the agency charged by Congress had begun to work. The agency had begun to encroach upon constituencies dear to congressmen. I have heard top officers of a department plot how best to force Congress to take responsibility for what Congress supposedly wanted because pressure "out there" was too intense for the department to handle. Excluded from this circuit of non-responsibility and evasion is the general citizenry in whose name all this is being done. The regulatory process, often binding lawmaker and bureaucrat in strategies of mutual incomprehension, leaves the absent citizenry cynical and dispirited. If someone tells me that this is how it works and one must take a "mature" or "pragmatic" view of it all, I can only reply that it is in fact not working in the best interests of the public; and that the public distrust of public servants, elected or appointed, has roots deeper than Watergate and many consequences no "insider" ought

107

lightly to dismiss. The regulatory process, viscous, dense and often dangerously intrusive, is its own worst enemy. No government, regardless of how well motivated it is, can paste up again the Garden of Eden.

It is also clear that this process is not always as mindless or closed as I have made it sound. The underlying intentions are laudable and desirable, and the defenders of the process, when confronted with the effects of their good intentions, should ask, pointedly: where *self*-regulation is so notably lacking, in the social and commercial world, what is the government to do? Is the government to be irresponsible, feckless, uninterested, withdrawn? Regulation, after all, is the only appropriate and serious response to a situation where any form of self-regulation, self-government, self-imposed sense of responsibility, is lacking. We may object to federal regulation but the government of the United States does promote important social goals, especially when certain segments of society have no strong interest in promoting them or when other deserving or disadvantaged segments of society lack the strength to promote them. After all, federal power and federal regulation were, and are, essential to the promotion of racial justice and the battle against discrimination in this country. Here federal regulation made, and makes, real the public interest. We may well speak of initiative and incentives and imagination and of how a free market or a free people need them, but if imagination and initiative and incentives are only

108

devoted to private purposes, then no responsible government can sit idly by if self-interest is not and will never be coincident with the public interest.

To preach of the public interest and to serve only one's private concerns, in a way that ignores the public interest, is to ask for regulation or for revolution, and a rational people would rather conduct its struggles through the political and judicial systems than in the streets. And yet, if we want a polity less split by competing pressures, less fragmented by interest groups adept in moralistic rhetoric and absolutistic posturing, then all parts of the private sector must become less suspicious of each other and more disposed to mutual cooperation and self-governance. Self-regulation for the public good within the private sector is the only way to convince the citizenry that it need not cry, or allow, for federal regulation. In all sectors, public and private, we desperately need in this country a greater concern for the public interest, and more sensitive understanding of the civic responsibilities of power. We all need to think better of ourselves and to act on the best of our common belief.

If such is the case against federal regulation and if such is the legitimate claim for federal regulation, then the challenge to the private, independent university and college is real and insistent. It is a fact that we depend upon federal help and are subjected to sullen waves of federal control. There is no denying that the federal government is in private university education. Basic research in the physical,

109

medical and many of the social sciences cannot go forward without federal help. Millions of young Americans cannot go to college or university, anywhere, for whatever purpose, without federal assistance. We must recognize that, and recognize that there is no question whatsoever that we must be accountable, in ways appropriate to the work we do, for the public's money. But we must also recognize that more than accountability has been agreed to. There is no point in simply lamenting that this is so, and that a bygone day, before the Second World War, is not with us now. The government's role in financing education is a fact and it cannot change. Nor should we assume that only evil flows from that fact; that all is lost and that our children will only own the ruins of a once noble private or independent edifice. A healthy, mutually beneficial relationship with government is within the private university's grasp.

It will not be easy to achieve such a relationship. To work toward one in the interests of the nation entails real risks, particularly if collaboration is pursued in an opportunistic fashion on either side, or is pursued by either party only for venal ends. To understand what is at risk and what must never be lost—indeed, what must be, for the nation's good, sustained—let us now turn to the private character of a private university.

The essence of that private character is in the university's independence. That independence, the most precious asset of any private university or college, is what we maintain for ourselves on behalf of America. In our independence, our self-interest as an institution serves and meets the nation's public interest. Assuming, therefore, our need to appreciate and yet responsibly resist the role of the federal government, the central question to pause on here is: in what does the independent character of a private university consist and how does that independent character contribute to America's needs?

In my view, the independent character of the private university is defined by the following features, the first of which obviously does not separate public from private universities but is common to them:

(I) The institution has, and must assert, as its central mission teaching, scholarship, and the dissemination of knowledge;

(II) The institution has, and must retain, the right to act as a fiduciary for itself;

(III) The institution has, and must defend, the right to define free inquiry for the truth for itself;

(IV) The institution has, and must maintain, the right to set standards for admission, for appointments and for the assessment of excellence, consistent with its human and intellectual values, for itself;

(V) The institution has, and must sustain,

111

the right to govern itself according to those traditions and values it has learned to cherish and defend and disseminate;

(VI) The institution has, and must promote, its civic role in supporting and strengthening the country's fundamental values through constructive criticism, open debate and freedom, within and without, from coercion of any kind.

Those are the features of the independent character of a private university. When federal intrusion (or anyone else's) threatens that independent character, that intrusion must be resisted. Because federal money brings federal control, however, and control is to be resisted because we and the country believe in and need private, independent centers of equity and excellence, money will have to come from other sources than the government. Institutions that do not have the capacity to make profits cannot subsist only on defiance, rhetoric and the aspiration to quality. Therefore one turns to the other part of the private sector, the corporate part, where the incentive and ability to make profit abounds. To that part of the private sector we say that if it does not support the not-for-profit part—the colleges and universities, the symphonies, the theaters, ballets, hospitals, the voluntary organizations—one of two things will happen. Either those enterprises will turn completely to the only source of funds large and accessible enough to support them in some measure, the federal government, or they will not survive. Either the not-for-profit part of the private sector will go to the government and make the best case for its contribution to the larger society, and will hope the society will listen, and then will live with the consequences of having been attended to, or the not-for-profit part of the private sector will cease to make its contributions, locally and nationally, in education, medicine, the arts, and will close up—in either case, cease as a private enterprise.

The corporate part of the private sector has a vital stake in the survival and in the vigorous health of the not-for-profit part. Speaking from the perspective of private universities, I see those universities and the corporate part of America as needing each other. They need each other not in some spirit of ideological collusion or social condescension but in order to sustain the principle that this country must have a variety of ways of solving its problems and of maintaining its basic values. A variety of institutions is necessary to further America's tradition of mutually collaborative, if differing, approaches to the public good. In linking the educational and corporate parts of the private sector, I am asserting two things: first, that each part is necessary to the health and responsible creativity of the other part; and second, that the private sector as a whole is essential to the health and imaginative energy of the nation as a whole.

Located by charter and tradition in its independent place between the corporate part of the private sector and the public realm of government, the private university also plays another role, a role essential in a pluralistic, free society. And that is the role of independent critic, critic of the private sector it inhabits, of the government it respects, of itself as an institution and as the guardian of a process. The historic exercise of that role by the private university has not always endeared it to others, nor has it rendered, nor should it ever render, the private university immune to the critical insights of others. The stimulation and criticism from the university able to exercise its independence are as often directed at the public sector, as they have been in these remarks, as much as at any other part of the society. The essential fact is that the capacity to be an independent, responsible voice, speaking its convictions in a fashion that does not take partisan political sides, has been very important to America and must continue to be important. When necessary, that voice should note the expansion of government control; when necessary, that voice should note the shortcomings of the academy or of other parts of the private sector. But it is always necessary, for the health of the rest of the society, that some institution in this country, and I believe it is the great, private university, sustain the reality of non-governmental solutions to the nation's needs, and do that by continuing to send out into the country men and women who understand and wish to strengthen the deeply important traditions of independence and pluralism that have so marked our country's history.

If the corporate part of America truly wants certain of its convictions set forth, in ways that insure the integrity of non-governmental alternatives, and the precious values of free inquiry, and of a life relatively unencumbered by federal regulation; if the corporate part of the private sector is really interested in a free market—of ideas—then it ought to act on its convictions, and support the not-for-profit part of the society. The corporate part of America may donate up to 5 percent of its taxable income to charity and then, such is the incentive offered by the federal government, write off the donation. Now, in fact, the corporate part of America averages .9 percent in its giving. The time has come to say it clearly: the private universities in this country know what they are and why they are valuable but they need support. They need support that does not require some political tilt or ideological coloration, for that would be to subvert what must be sustained, but support that believes in the competition of ideas and in the need to sustain centers of excellence that can define excellence for themselves, on behalf of the nation, without bureaucratic or political interference.

Private universities must, in the first instance, support themselves. They must have as well the support of the rest of the private sector; and if they truly act in the nation's interest and abide by the norms of the public's trust, they deserve the help of a government devoted as well to that national interest and public trust. There are, however, many forms of support in addition to financial assistance. There is also the support that stems from understanding and from recognizing common obligations. Twenty years ago the private, and public, research universities were turned into centers for federally sponsored research. Now the government seems singularly unwilling to admit what it has done or to acknowledge what massive good on behalf of the American people flowed from that act. There is no willingness or capacity to say that having engaged educational institutions on behalf of the people, for research on space, cancer, energy, and thousands of other problems, that we are better for it, or that an important relationship has begun to be forged in the nation's interest, or that now mutual respect for how work is done must be shown if something larger, the nation's sense of purpose, is to remain strong. A university is built to remember; the government too often is seized by amnesia. Good faith between them is not the result, and that is what the country conspicuously lacks.

It is now a political season and candidates and their legionnaires are thick on the ground. There is no support for the historic importance of independent, research institutions from them. Indeed, there is not yet one aspirant or former aspirant for the presidency of the United States, or any other national office, who has said *anything* about education in general. We have not yet heard anyone speak to that process of instruction in skills and values that touches every American family in some part; that single concern, education, that in every community

116

in the land and in most American homes can inflame tension and passion and hope as few religious and political issues can. We hear no candidate recognize that with inflation and unemployment, education, its costs and its rewards, is at the heart of the domestic matter for Americans, and that indeed education is critically affected by and critically affects all the issues that are talked about. We hear nothing about the basic process we have defined historically as essential to a free citizenry, a process that has as much to do with overcoming poverty and violence and structural unemployment and a sense of national listlessness as anything in the country.

I know there is a new Department of Education in Washington. Its creation in no way speaks to a concern for the quality of education in this country. And no politician has been so graceless as to pretend that it does. I repeat: at a time of increasing national bafflement and chagrin, I hear nothing from the politicians about making America more confident, more cohesive, more capacious, better, through making education, public or private, better. Yet America has thought long and hard on the proposition that education is essential to a free, productive, flourishing democracy. We all know that education is thought by the country to be crucial to the future of the country. And we have heard nothing of it, in any form, from the candidates. What will they say, what will the leaders of the corporate part of America say and do to sustain what is so clearly in the nation's interest? For our part, we have asserted again, as we have before, the nature, purpose and character of a private, independent center of learning, of a university; and we assert again the need for these private institutions to pursue their own supportive, collaborative, independent path for the nation's good. What we have asserted stems from two principled convictions: that all private institutions, however defined, are needed by this country, and that independent status is necessary in a free society where alternatives and excellence and equality of opportunity for all must also be at one.

Science and the University

There are both difficulties and challenges of doing basic research in science in a research university. Basic research is not, of course, confined to the activity of scientists. Basic research, that is, investigation that seeks new knowledge and understanding rather than solutions to immediate problems, is the essential nature of research on the part of all scholars. It obviously includes but is not restricted to basic research in the biological, medical, physical and many social sciences. In the sciences, however, there is a particular style to the enterprise. Teaching in these areas, done in laboratories, in groups or teams, through colloquia, on field trips; with undergraduates, graduate and post-doctoral students, with assistants and associates in research, is intimately and inextricably connected to research. In science, teaching and research not only go hand in hand, they are often the same hand; the pedagogical act an act of investigation, the investigatory act shared with students and associates who are also colleagues, the whole a splendid, ongoing instance of intellectual and human collaboration. Of course scientists also work alone. Not all that is done is the result of a group effort; and not everything that is done occurs in a unified act that is both pedagogical and investigatory. But the distinctive style of scientific investigation is collaborative, and the distinctive process is such that it is impossible finally to distinguish research from teaching, seeking from sharing.

The dollars involved in supporting and furthering this kind of basic research are immense. They are largely federal dollars, which is to say taxpayers' dollars. In constant 1972 dollars, the government spent $2.8 billion on basic research in 1978, up $1.8 billion since 1960, when the reaction to Sputnik was in full flight. In 1958, 32 percent of all basic research in America was done in universities; by 1978, 52 percent was being done in universities. And in those universities, in 1978, 72 percent of the money for basic research came from the federal government. The result of this federal support to university-based science has been tremendous improvements in the life of America's citizens. In health care, in the production of food, in the handling of information—in the quality of our life— our government has brought about massive benefits by encouraging science and scientific research in universities.

The federal money that comes to universities brings with it money for the support of the administration of these complex projects; it brings reimbursements for "indirect costs." Indirect costs, or overhead, provide reimbursement for expenses which cannot be accurately assessed for each research project. They include, therefore, reimbursements for part of Yale's cost of heating, cooling and maintaining research laboratories, as well as for part of the cost of essential supporting services like accounting and purchasing. Finally, these reimbursements bear part of the price of meeting federal requirements in certain areas: affirmative action, bio-safety, the protection of human subjects and the like. In 1960, Yale received some $24 million in federal funds, $3 million of which was indirect cost money; in fiscal year 1980, Yale received $68 million in federal money, $21 million of which was in indirect costs. Thus about 30 percent of the total operating budget of the university—a great deal of money, though not a particularly high percentage compared to others with whom we compete—comes from the government.

It was not difficult for the government in the last twenty years partially to turn universities into installations for federally sponsored basic research in space, cancer, agriculture, energy and a thousand other areas. The scientists were delighted to have their work supported and appreciated; the university administrators were delighted to have science expand and, with the additional monies garnered, to have their institutions generally supported and made bigger. Everyone benefited. While the money was flowing, while there were ample pools of students, while energy was seemingly cheap, while facilities could be expanded or renovated and instrumentation and space could be acquired, all seemed well.

The welcome streams of federal money for research, however, opened the channels for a mounting wave of regulation, and there are now at least fifty-nine federal laws and regulations that govern or affect scientific research in universities, according to the editorial in the April 25, 1980 issue of *Science*. Federal regulation is not, *prima facie*, evil. The obligation of the government to protect those citizens who cannot protect themselves—as in all the civil rights legislation—is unquestioned. The obligation of the government to account for money it collects from its citizens, and to require accurate accounting from those to whom the money is extended on behalf of the people, is unquestioned. I raise the issue of federal regulation not at all to object to regulation in principle, but to object to it as a set of processes; I do not object to the need for regulation in certain circumstances, or to the obligation to regulate, but rather to how regulation often works. I am proud of a government that promotes equity in human affairs and in matters of the marketplace. I am appalled, however, by the requirements for massive amounts of paperwork; by uncoordinated or special interest mandates that promote social goods with no awareness of the costs to other social goods; by an unwillingness or inability on the part of regulators to recognize legitimate and necessary distinctions among social entities being regulated. I believe in regulation but not in leveling all distinctions and issues. The City of God is desirable but it does not occur when a landscape consists of evenly distributed rubble.

Because of excessive or unthinking regulation, the relationship between government and universities is seriously damaged. There is powerful resentment on all sides, and distrust. Goodwill is eroded dangerously, and a strain very old and very deep in our culture—a radical skepticism bordering on open contempt for our centers of learning with their strange, haughty ways—surfaces again. In general, federal agencies and universities find each other incomprehensible in structure, obdurate in attitude, intractable in negotiation. This recent and growing schism between government and universities is not created by science but it deeply affects the capacity to do science.

It is time for a concrete example. I choose the one summarized across this country in the scientific research community by the designation A-21.

Two and a half years ago, when I first heard of it, I thought A-21 was a vitamin. I was wrong. A-21 refers to that circular from the Office of Management and Budget entitled "Cost Principles for Educational Institutions" published in the *Federal Register* on March 6, 1979. In it, the government proposes means to account for its money. It wishes to know if the money is used for the purpose for which it was given, and if direct and indirect monies are properly accounted for. The principle of accountability, as I have said, is not at issue. What is at issue is *how* the accountability will be accomplished. The Office of Management and Budget says in A-21 that there must be "activity" or "total workload" documentation, and that faculty members on federal grants or contracts must report their workload or effort in multiple categories—research, teaching, service, administration.* These discrete categories must be reported in terms of percentages, and these percentages must add up to 100 percent. Like many others, I object—on the following grounds:

that some individuals in the government must believe the government fully owns a principal investigator and that it has a right to require documentation of that person's "workload" even when that work is unconnected with federally sponsored work;

that some individuals in the government must misunderstand completely that it is impossible

* "Each report will account for 100 percent of the activity for which the employee is compensated and which is required in fulfillment of the employee's obligations to the institution. The report will reasonably reflect the percentage of activity applicable to each sponsored agreement, each indirect cost category, and each major function of the institution." Paragraph J.6.

to segregate teaching from research from administration in doing basic research and to assign precise percentages to these false distinctions;

that such requirements to create false categories will inevitably result in reports which are wholly meaningless and may only bury, not reveal, genuine instances of improper use of federal money.

These requirements, and objections, are not new. This circular, issued on September 10, 1958 by the then Bureau of the Budget, was revised in the summer of 1967 when the Bureau introduced new amendments to A-21 which would have required detailed segmenting and documentation of faculty effort. The intensity of the outcry against those regulations led to the formation of a task force, chaired by Cecil Goode, of the Bureau of the Budget, to examine the issue. After extensive interviews involving twenty-two universities and more than 350 individuals, mostly faculty, a report, "Time or Effort Reporting by Colleges and Universities in Support of Research Grants and Contracts," was made public in February 1968. The first of its five recommendations began: "For professorial staff, drop the requirement for effort reports contained in the present [1967] Circular A-21" and the first two of its six conclusions read *in toto:*

"1. Time or effort reports now required of faculty members are meaningless and a waste of time.

They have engendered an emotional reaction in the academic community that will endanger university-federal relations if relief is not provided. They foster a cynical attitude toward the requirements of government and take valuable effort away from more important activities, not the least of which is the research involved.

"2. We need to go to a system that does not require documentary support of faculty time devoted to government-sponsored research. No real evidence of faculty effort is provided anyway under the present system, and there is no way to prove how much effort was in fact expended."

Those sentiments are as valid now as they were in 1968. Was the task force co-opted or stacked? Was it subverted by "emotional" academic members? No. The bottom of the title page tells us it is "A Report by a Task Force Comprised of Representatives from:

Bureau of the Budget
General Accounting Office
Department of Defense
National Science Foundation
Department of Health, Education, and Welfare"

Relevant officials of the government advised against the proposed regulations. As a result circular A-21 was revised and the objectionable requirements on "effort" reporting were dropped. Did the government forget its own study? Yes. In 1976, the Department of Health, Education and Welfare redrafted A-21 and in general reconstituted those features against which the government task force had so strongly advised.

Subsequent negotiations on the subject of "workload" documentation between universities, the Office of Management and Budget and the Department of Health, Education and Welfare accountants availed little. History was completely ignored, the most terrifying mistake of the mind an individual or a government can make. The Office of Management and Budget was also indifferent to recent events. A private and independent effort to satisfy the need for accountability and to salvage the decomposing relationship between government and the universities in the area of sponsored basic research resulted in the creation of a National Commission on Research. Its membership included outstanding individuals from the American Association for the Advancement of Science, major private corporations, universities, research institutes and foundations. In February 1980, it published the first of a projected series of reports: "Accountability: Restoring the Quality of the Partnership." The title is admirably descriptive of the basic issues.

Among other recommendations, the National Commission on Research spoke directly to the issues of effort reporting. In these and other areas, it asserts the need for proper accountability and sets forth rational, tough, workable grounds for sharing the responsibility as well as the funds. Many urged these recommendations on the Office of Management and Budget. Nothing came of the urging. In October 1979 A-21 went into effect. Then in early fall of 1980 the Office of Management and Budget approved, on an experimental basis, a method of statistical sampling designed to provide accountability in a much less intrusive fashion for the scientists involved, and to yield much more accurate and realistic information for the government agencies. I hope this method is designed to work. I hope that with regard to documentation of "total workload" the Office of Management and Budget does not remain forever enthralled by its own regulatory rhetoric. We will see. In the meantime, never have I seen the lash of federal regulation applied to a crucial area of the nation's intellectual life with such seeming indifference to financial and human consequences. In its issue of October 3, 1980, *Science* estimated that at Stanford University alone, these new regulations would require an increase from 3,000 to 80,000 reports annually, and $250,000 to $300,000 to put in place the new reporting system. It has been a long and deeply disheartening series of events, wasteful of energy and faith and time.

On so many other matters touching basic research, President Carter's administration demonstrated its awareness at the highest levels that basic scientific research carried out in universities is essential to the productivity and the long-term revitalization of many segments of America's economy. Indeed, the most recent statement of this recognition of the mix of teaching and research in the furtherance of

128

science was clearly made by Vice-President Mondale in a speech at MIT on September 25, 1980. Below the highest levels, however, this spirit and vision have not prevailed. I hope the vision will prevail, because what is at stake is the quality of American science and, therefore, of a free, stable, productive nation.

What is needed? Aside from the issues involved in A-21 or any other specific set of regulations, we continue to need leadership capable of transcending special interests and seeing—whole—the public interest. Whether in the areas of basic research or of financing higher education; whether around regulations concerning safety or athletics or informed consent or waste disposal, there must be no lessening of the moral imperatives, or of necessary accountability. But there must be at all levels of government, and the university, some renewed mutual respect, some common conviction that it is in the nation's interest that government and centers of learning collaborate, and that the purpose of collaboration is the betterment of the nation's life. There must be some disposition to identify the larger issues and find reasonable solutions within a general perspective that recognizes institutional differences and common goals. Too much is at stake for all of us.

What will Yale do? We will continue to press for open discussion and for the responsibilities of the University, its responsibility to be accountable, its responsibility to protect the integrity of its faculty and the independence of its mission. We will volunteer to be part of the experiment of statistical sampling meant to show that there is a simpler yet sound approach to accountability. We will continue to work for collaboration. That is, after all, our very essence.

In restoring a partnership with the government we will call upon alumni to help make our case; as citizens of the country, as members of the Yale family, they can help in this task, and I will ask for help. We must also increasingly rely on faculty for assistance. Through no fault of theirs, members of the faculty have far too seldom been asked by universities to participate in the policy-oriented conversations with the government on matters which profoundly affect their ability to do research and to share their knowledge and discoveries with others. Not only is faculty often expert in the areas I have identified but there is a deeper, more searing problem to be addressed. Unintentionally, the government and its regulations have set faculties against administrations. Had the government wished to split universities internally it could not have found a better way than to make administrators custodians of regulations they do not necessarily accept, and make faculty the bearers of the burden of frustrated resistance. The collegial nature of our institutions of learning is our driving ideal, a unique asset; it cannot be imperiled. There are pressures enough on universities without allowing federal regulations to sunder us.

And we will continue to encourage appropriate links between the private corporate sector and the University, in order to find alternate sources of money, and to seek new sources of intellectual stimulation, for university scientists. Collaboration is not a concept to be confined to the relationship with the federal government. Such collaboration will be far from easy. There is still, despite all the new talk of such relationships, a ballet of distrust and defensiveness between universities and the corporate world. And there are genuine risks. The dangers we have seen in the various forms of federal intrusion cannot be exchanged for other kinds of intrusion from the private, corporate sector. Neither is allowable. One is not preferable to the other. The norms of University research remain and must remain those of free access to information, independent assessment of evidence, the capacity freely to publish results subject to review of peers. To those who fear that the private sector will impose requirements on the University which would violate the academic integrity and processes that lie at the heart of our place, I say I understand the concern and will not ever dismiss it. No money offered from any quarter that would require inappropriate promises or behavior will be accepted.

My experience is that the private sector tends to understand and respect the norms and values of a private university far better than the federal government. Private corporations have after all their own private corporate norms too; conversations between them and universities quickly establish the lines each entity must respect and protect. Private corporations do not have the capacity to follow their money with coercive regulations unconnected with anything else. They do not forget from administration to administration, or from department to department, what they have said.

Understanding all this, however, I do not propose to see the values and integrity of the University compromised. I do intend to explore relationships, with any part of our society with whom we can appropriately and honorably collaborate, and I intend to explore such relationships in possession of our principles, mindful of the history of our federal relations, sensitive always to the fact that the university is an independent institution in our society, and that it cannot serve society responsibly unless that independence is its paramount concern.

The problems I have discussed are not glamorous and brightly colored; their solutions are not simple or to be magically derived from a single source. They are gritty, grainy problems that involve hundreds of hours of work, thousands of details, millions of words, endless pieces of paper. They are deeply important problems, however, not because of the details or even the dollars but because they speak to how science is done. They speak to what the future holds for America's capacity to improve its productivity and economic vitality and to improve the quality of its citizens' lives through science and technology. The issues of collaboration, regulation and independent integrity also pierce to the center of the whole process of apprehending and comprehending the world we live in, the worlds we are, that is the essence of science as it is of everything else we do in the university.

Science is at the core of the University's mission to foster the disciplined imagination. Whatever strikes at that core cuts at the heart of the University.

The American Teacher

A liberal education is at the heart of a civil society, and at the heart of a liberal education is the act of teaching. To speak directly of how a liberal education prepares students for a civic role, we must begin with the teacher.

The teacher chooses. The teacher chooses how to structure choice. The teacher's power and responsibility lie in choosing where everyone will begin and how, from that beginning, the end will be shaped. The choice of that final form lies in the teacher's initial act. The phrase "final form" sounds more arbitrary and imposing than it should. No good teacher ever wants to control the contour of another's mind. That would not be teaching, it would be a form of terrorism. But no good teacher wants the contour of another's mind to be blurred. Somehow the line be-

134

tween encouraging a design and imposing a specific
stamp must be found and clarified. That is where
the teacher first begins to choose.

In selecting what will be taught, in that lifetime
of selecting, the teacher decides what is first important, what skein of implications and affiliations and
hints and directions waits to be woven. And in choosing where to begin, all these choices begin to be
displayed, if only to the mind that hopes they will
exist. Teaching is an instinctual art, mindful of potential, craving of realizations, a pausing, seamless
process, where one rehearses constantly while act-
ing, sits as a spectator at a play one directs, engages
every part in order to keep the choices open and the
shape alive for the student, so that the student may
enter in, and begin to do what the teacher has done:
make choices.

These impressions of teaching will doubtless
strike many as too unspotted by reality. In this account, there is no bad weather, no child at home
with strep throat. There is no unprepared teacher.
There is no recognition that students, or teachers
or books, can be boring or deeply garbled. I have
projected a process of choice and shape as if teaching were really what the ancients and their Renaissance emulators said it was, a sculpting process,
whereby the clay or stone or wax, inorganic material but malleable, could, through choices, be made
to take a shape that nature never saw, a shape art
supplies to the stuff the world provides. While I do
not think teaching is as painless or effortless as I

may have made it sound, I do believe it is essentially the ethical and aesthetic activity I propose. I do believe it involves the making and setting of right and wrong choices in the interests of a larger, shaping process, and that the deep thrill a teacher can experience comes from the combination of these activities, so that you feel what you think, do what you talk about, judge as you talk about judgment, proceed logically as you reveal logical structure, clarify as you talk about clarity, reveal as you show what nature reveals—all in the service of encouraging the student in imitation and then repetition of the process you have been summoning, all so that the student may turn himself not into you but into himself.

No human activity can proceed without making choices—critical acts of the mind—and teaching, which embraces any subject or discipline, is about how to make a choice. That is the ethical impulse in teaching—to tell how to go about acquiring the material and then building the edifice of a belief. And from the architectonics of choices a person will emerge, a person who knows how to cope with the radical loneliness we all inherit and the vast population of decisions we all live in, a person who can carry on.

If choosing is what the teacher does and wants the student to learn to do, choosing is that which also binds them, teacher and student, and binds us all, each to one another. It is not the only thing, but it is an essential thing. How we choose to believe

136

and speak and treat others, how we choose a civic role for ourselves, is the deepest purpose of a liberal education and of the act of teaching.

Teaching is an emblem of our civic life because teaching is, in every sense of the word, a deeply conventional act, that is, an act of convening, sanctioned by usage, for the purpose of making a covenant. In an agreed-upon context it brings together minds so that a second agreement may be struck and acted upon, an agreement that there is, for the sustenance of our lives, a shared principle of sharing. Teaching is an assertion of the common capacity of the human mind to make and sustain a context in which another mind makes back, and thus makes anew. In the mutuality of minds—which does not necessarily mean agreement or acquiescence or domination —there is a recognition of mutual receptivity. And in the receptivity there is, every time, every day, everywhere, another example of the way human minds can find a common ground and clear it and build a city where people live together.

In this civic sense, teaching is a political act in that it seeks to construe a polity, defined by shared responsibility and authority. Every classroom is an act of making citizens in the realm of that room, and every room is a figure for the larger community. And the purpose of that activity—beyond the content of the class or the subject matter or discipline, regardless of at what "level" the activity occurs—is the perpetuation of how knowledge is acquired and shared and made perpetual. When in canto XV of

137

the *Inferno* Dante meets his old teacher Brunetto
Latini, he says to Brunetto that the old man "*M'in-
segnavate come l'uom s'etterna*"; he says, with respect and affection, "You taught me how a person
makes himself eternal." Beneath the fact that Brunetto, minor poet, taught Dante, God's scribe, how
writing poetry allows us to outlast time, is a deeper
perception. And that is how teaching is self-perpetu-
ation, perpetuation of the self in the students who find
themselves; a perpetuation not of blood nor even of
similarity, but a disinterested perpetuation, a giving
to others the gift of how to share their desire that
humankind survive as it should, with dignity and
energy and moral purpose. At its best, teaching must
lead us out of ourselves, into a shared understanding
that our hope for a decent, civilized life depends for
its very existence upon others sharing the same hope.

I wish to speak of teaching in a civil society because I have sensed for some time how under-valued
the profession of teaching has been. Here is the
shadow in my subject. Teachers, in grammar or high
schools, in colleges or universities, in places large
and small, public and private, new or old, have never
truly been cherished by this country in a way that is
equal to the importance the country so clearly at-
taches to them. An excessive assertion? Consider
some of the folk-myths or popular images America
clings to about teachers.

There is the vision of the one-room school house,

once a reality, now a fact in only remote parts of the country. It is, however, still a benign image, burnished by nostalgia—particularly by those who never knew one—because it seems such a perfect form of the collaborative society. Then there is a more problematic figure, the mythical splendid spinster, the "school marm," a version of the Minerva Armata, the single-minded, much corsetted, always middle-aged female, childless and endlessly maternal, whose role in society was to take care of its children without having any of her own, a figure meant to teach man how to make himself eternal but springing full-grown herself from the Jovian brow of Normal School. That mythical figure begins to tell us that in America, teaching is "female," or at best androgynous, a necessary art whose potency must be contained. And kept peripheral.

The college teacher, who is my special focus, in popular myth is a bumbler, prey to malign influences because he is so innocent, a figure unfit for the rigors of what is still constantly called "the real world," as if schools at any level were not real, or were not part of the reality of America. At best the popular image of the college teacher, endlessly retailed by television or popular literature, is that of a rumpled child, fit to tend his grazing herd of adolescents across academic groves but totally lost before machines, money and worldly temptation. He is always dressed out of season, often has an accent, and he is, if anything, more peripheral and weaker than the frontier woman who teaches below him in the system. If she was your maiden aunt, he is her pale brother.

Popular images are caricatures, their heightened features reflecting society's submerged convictions. Perhaps we should ignore them, but that would be to ignore ourselves, and how we think of the teacher. At bottom, these images and their variants show us figures who have either never been out there or who have retreated back in here, and who in both cases do not really do anything. They go to class but not to the office. They meet neither trains, payrolls nor the public; what they sell cannot be seen and probably, therefore, does not exist. If it does, it is suspect.

Beyond caricature, there are other misapprehensions. There is, for instance, a widespread conviction that college and university teachers seem to require a peculiar form of job security, called tenure. Such has been the result of the academic community's remarkable lack of success in communicating the nature of its work. Academe has never persuaded the society at large that tenure is not job security only, as it can (perhaps improperly) be construed in civil services or labor unions or the partnerships of law firms, but that it is the manifestation of a principle called academic freedom, a principle that says one must have the right, responsibly, freely to pursue and express the truth as one sees it. The principle of academic freedom is not intended to buffer incompetence in teaching from the consequences of an open, competitive marketplace of ideas. Tenure, embodying in a word a principle and a whole set of policies for its assumption, is not a perfect device for the protection of the free inquiry into the truth. But tenure is essential to the ideal of free inquiry and that ideal is the essence of the mission of a college or university in a free society. Have we strayed from our subject? I think not. The role of the teacher is linked to the nature of the institution in which the teaching is performed, and to the nature of the society that the institution serves.

The popular view of the marginality of certain types of teachers has traditionally found its response in academic hauteur, in college and university teachers' over-reacting to a sense of marginality by asserting a view of themselves as a mandarin class. This new class believed that if society would not value them, even as it sent them society's young, then they would scorn a society that entrusted its future to those it treated as servants. Academic people in America have often felt under-valued and therefore have tended to over-appreciate themselves. It would have been better to assert the central value of the profession rather than to claim more for professors than anyone, particularly they themselves, in their heart of hearts, would have been willing to grant.

In short, college teachers in this country have often been defensive and at times have allowed teaching to go undefended. And in the last twenty-five to thirty years in America certain events that have had a direct impact on how college and university teachers believe themselves viewed by the larger society have not enhanced either the academic profession's estimate of itself or the society's judgment of the profession. I refer specifically to the era of Senator Joseph McCarthy in the 1950s and to the period of the student disturbances in the mid-1960s and early 1970s. In both cases, the academic profession, in the first instance more as individuals, in the second as individuals involved in a certain activity, felt itself under assault. Regardless of the precise issues, in both periods there lingered, within colleges and universities and without, a sense of misplacement and incapacity. Whether the code word was subversion or irrelevance; whether the epithets were egghead or pointy head or Archie Bunker's meathead; whether the insult to the body of the academy was coming from the center of government or from the center of the campus—which is to say, from the citizenry—it was an assault on those who had chosen in some form to make with their minds, and it reminded the teacher of his supposedly marginal status.

There were those teachers and others who resented this view, which they knew to be false but which they believed to be the inevitable consequence of certain strains in the culture; there were others who embraced this view, their reason being that if such were the centers, they would gladly be eccentric; if such were the inhumane values of a senator or the SDS, they wanted none of it. But when the waving of lists and of placards passed, when the similar sloganeering of right and left had grown hoarse and was discredited, when ideological frenzy had revealed itself as a lust for personal power masquerading as the public good, what was left? A profession remained which had never relied upon politicians for approbation but that had never before suffered the opprobrium of students. A profession survived which, while never counting on society's smile from the center of political power for a sense of reward, had always counted on and now had lost the center it always knew best, the students. A profession survived but baffled, shocked. The profession that McCarthy and The Movement said had betrayed its deepest obligations to the country and contemporary society now felt itself in the early 1970s more isolated than ever, made up of people more alone than anyone elsewhere could know. It was a profession that, in secret ways, at recesses that no one talked much about, had lost something more than the approval of the world; it had lost that without which none of us can be effective as people at all, its sense of self-respect and self-esteem, its sense of dignity. What was left behind was uncertainty, anger, at worst self-hatred.

I leave out of this account the complex matrix of causes and motive that historians and sociologists and cultural analysts can and will adduce. I give you the view of one who by circumstances of background and choice has seen the past quarter century or more of academic life close up. I describe the growth of a sensibility; no more. But I can trace the growth of a crisis of confidence in the academy, and particularly at the heart of it. I can note the gathering conviction that the act and activity of teaching, which for me includes finally research and investigation and civic effort, is not viewed by those who do it or who would do it with the degree of faith in it as a noble calling, important to the country, as they must if it is to be done as well as it must be on behalf of the country. It is one thing to know others questioned your worth and the worth of the subject matter you professed; it is much more serious when because of them and other recent events you question your worth and the worth of what you do as a teacher in an area of intellectual inquiry, and begin to lose all faith.

The economic contractions now spreading deeper and deeper in every institution of higher learning in this country come, therefore, at the end of a long series of events. The gradual expansion of research monies and students and faculty and physical plant in the last twenty years is not the only backdrop against which to see the issues within the college and university teaching profession. To understand the perturbations of soul nationally in the teaching profession only against economic issues in the last two decades falsifies the picture; a truer perspective is one that sees the various patterns of economic growth and contraction within the context of a vocational crisis in the academic profession, a crisis which has been going on much longer and cuts a much deeper wound.

What does one do? In addition to understanding this crisis and constantly making its consequences the prism through which one regards the spiritual health of the liberal arts and professional educational process, there are several things one must do.

The first thing is to act on one's conviction that excellence is transmitted within colleges and universities (and all other schools) through individuals. This conviction places the quality and well-being of the faculty as the most important of all the issues facing us in education for the next difficult years. Such a conviction, when acted upon, means making every effort, extraordinary and other, at least to pay the faculty at a level commensurate with its dedication and its excellence and its dignity. It means putting the genuine needs of the people who teach at the center of the institution's concerns, for they are the heart of the place; they perform the essential activity of the place, without which no educational institution exists, and through which the quality of the place, and hence of the nation's life, is maintained and made better.

The second thing to do is never to lose sight of the special needs of the younger faculty, those in the profession already and those who are about to enter it. Swooping demographic curves, economic forecasts about inflation, government laws concerning retirement, statistics about the lack of new jobs for Ph.D.s between 1983 and 1989, the perceptible patterns of young faculty leaving teaching for other professions or of people refusing to leave other professions to enter teaching, projections about "a lost generation of scholars," or the quality of the pool of applicants of those still choosing to go to graduate school—all such measures and indicators tell only the surface of the narrative. The deeper text tells of the longer-range problem, the ferocious frustration and feeling of futility experienced by many young people when the profession, the way of life, that they love with all their being cannot or will not return the devotion in any measure. The feeling of disproportion, the belief that one is playing as hard as possible in a game where the rules are suspended, the visceral feeling of the unfairness of it all, when all one wants is a chance to do one's job, exceeds anything felt by the younger people in my profession since the Depression. Again, the solutions can be envisaged, are difficult to implement, but necessary to find. One must never lose sight of the basic need of all institutions, and particularly educational ones which are intended every year to welcome new students, to bring new and vital people into them; one cannot lose sight of those who will lead the teaching profession into the next century; one must find and encourage and reward the best of them, by paying them well, by appreciating their teaching, their scholarly work, their engagement in the institution's general life, by finding them time to take leave to pursue their research, by keeping the faith with them, by never forgetting.

There is also something else one can do, with the younger faculty and the older, something that assumes the economic needs of all people who teach in today's inflationary time, and knows the brutal pressures on the young and the others, and that speaks to the deepest spiritual issues of a sense of self-worth and dignity and to the calling of teaching itself. One can say again, and ask you never to forget, regardless of what you do and where you go, that those who teach have done something without which most people could not do for themselves whatever it is they do; that the act of teaching is an exemplary act, of self-fashioning on behalf of knowledge that teaches others how to fashion the self; that no teacher is due more respect or affection than he or she has earned but that the drive behind the teaching effort is a positive one. It is a drive for civic engagement that in innumerable ways, through millions of individuals, over a period of time that embraces generations, results in the transmission of the values and standards and new knowledge in all forms that a society must have if it is to be civilized.

Does that sound too grandiose? I do not believe it is, for that statement simply recognizes the central importance, regardless of context or content or subject, of those who have made the very first choice teachers make. They have chosen, every day, to make themselves vulnerable, vulnerable to those others who are the future, in order to make what is made by the mind eternal. The human race survives despite itself in many ways, but it survives because of itself when it passes on the best of its past and the best of its aspiration through the open sharing of the blood and sinew of the mind. That moment of poise, when what is known becomes accessible and must then become what is to be found, is the act of teaching, and those acts in sequence are a life, in which, once we learn how, we are all teachers and students of ourselves. Those who choose to renew constantly those moments of poise with their lives, throughout their lives, are not by that choice an elect or a race apart. They are vessels as are others. But the teachers do believe they have a gift for giving; it drives them with the same irrepressible drive that drives other to create a work of art or a market or a building. It is the instinct to give shape to what constantly needs shaping so that others may have contour and meaning to their own lives that tells the true teacher that there is nothing else to be done with one's life but teach.

I think we are in a time when those who teach are wary of what they do, wary in a new way which is the result of twenty-five years or more of uncertainty and bafflement. We are in a time when the teachers, particularly the younger ones, are increasingly and distressingly accustomed to defining themselves, and hearing themselves defined negatively, that is, in terms of what they do not do, as well as pejoratively. I write, therefore, as someone who notes his own convictions regarding what teaching is, and why it can never be viewed as anything less than what it is, lest we allow mythology and frustration to displace a reality without which our country cannot flourish.

148

The American School

The stretching of instruction into citizenship is my theme. The nation's public schools are the arena of my concern. I believe in the central role of education in the formation and sustenance of a free and democratic nation, and I believe, therefore, in an education that has those civic goals as its end. Such a belief does not presume a preference for one kind of education over another. It rather assumes excellence as the driving energy toward the goal of a decent and productive life with others. My basic text, embodying these ideals, derives from a great book on elementary education, *Positions*, written in 1581 by the greatest of Elizabethan schoolmasters, Richard Mulcaster. The following passage sets forth the essential faith in education brought by the first settlers in the New World; it represents as its core the beliefs Jefferson would hold dear:

> "Education," said Mulcaster, "is the bringing up of one, not to live alone, but amongst others . . . whereby he shall be best able to execute those doings in life, which the state of his calling shall employ him unto, whether public abroad or private at home, according unto the direction of his country; whereunto he is born, and owes his whole service."

Public and private here refer to ourselves and the roles we choose for ourselves, all tending toward the enhancement of the common life we live with others. In America, the burden for that set of values, whose undergirding is a set of intellectual skills, has rested with the public school system, which is sustained by and responsive to the thousands of localities throughout the land. It is to those localities and the schools within them that I address myself, for to speak of excellence in education without some firm idea of the goal of excellence, and the historic traditions of that goal, would only compound our present confusion.

Our confusion stems from our worries about the state of our schools. It is compounded of anger, fear and frustration, and stems from our anxiety that there is in our schools across the country a situation bordering on endemic collapse.

The condition of many of the nation's elementary and high schools is worrisome enough; the conviction on the part of many Americans about the lack of quality and stability in the nation's public schools is even more worrisome. Whether the schools are as decayed as many people believe is not at all as clear as is the public's belief that the schools are a disaster.

Much of the anxiety derives from beliefs most Americans hold: that throughout our country's history school has been thought essential to a productive citizenry and stable society; that schooling is the responsibility equally of family and community; that the federal government has played a vital role in encouraging schools, from academies to land-grant universities, but that the federal government does not interfere with education at the local level, has not set up either a national school system or a national university; and that while the government, through the courts, has enforced a number of socially useful or desirable legal decisions within the schools, regarding integration of the races or freedom of belief, it has acted in accordance with the legal authority of the federal constitution, not from a desire to impede local values or lawful local traditions or differences. Beneath the fascinating tangle of local and national obligations and prerogatives that the public schools present, there runs a basic belief in America that education in this officially secular society is an almost sacred process, a process meant to open opportunity, promote access and mobility,

151

foster excellence, recognize merit, do all that urges Americans to make themselves productive, free and equal.

It is when this constellation of potentially contradictory beliefs and systems is ignored that concern increases. Beneath the layers of anxiety that our schools are riddled with truancy, absenteeism, dropping out and violence; that all the standard measures indicate a decline in the national ability to read and write and reckon; that teachers have lost their dedication and students their motivation and the whole system its quality, is the deepest anxiety: that no one is paying attention. The fear that local political leaders do nothing to assert the critical priority of the local schools; that national leaders retreat to bureaucratic bunkers or simply fail to acknowledge the plight of the schools, terrifies the people, particularly when the people know in their blood that somehow schools and education are still linked to jobs, economic growth and productivity, and a decent public order. The people believe those linkages but hear nothing about them from public officials, elected or appointed. And so the confusion grows until it is not hysterical but necessary to ask: what will happen to *all* young Americans' access to the American educational dream if the public schools fail or falter?

I think this question is one of the most pressing for our country at this century's end. I have no easy answer to it but I do have an attitude toward how to approach the question. At the root of that attitude is a distinction which I have made implicitly and must make explicit. That is the distinction I will argue America has long made between education and school. Although these terms and what they mean have often been bound or found together, the concepts are not necessarily synonymous. Indeed, to anticipate my argument, I believe our present confusion derives from the fact that the historic differences between the meanings of "education" and "school," and the tension engendered by those differences, have been lost. And in losing that tension between different concepts we have been left with distinct and unconnected memories masquerading as institutions; all tension, and therefore all meaning, gone.

What are those different meanings and what was the useful, indeed necessary, tension between them? First the meanings. From the beginning of our life as a people under a single government, "education" has been the means to assert an intellectual and civic ideal. While never occurring as a term or a concept in the Declaration of Independence or in the Constitution, education nevertheless appeared to the framers of those public assertions of principle as the essential process to promote the Republic's national ideals of civic harmony, general happiness, and collective freedom. Education was the means to creating the public good.

"Schools," however, are referred to in public documents from the earliest colonial period. In April 1642 the General Court of Massachusetts Bay asserted that because of "the great neglect of many

153

parents & masters in training up their children in learning & labor, & other implyments which may be proffitable to the common wealth," there must be henceforth in every town men to teach the children "to read & understand the principles of religion & capitall lawes of this country." The General Court could confidently mandate training in skills and values, labor and learning, because there was no fissure between schools and their larger purposes.

Five years later, the same assembly passed the first law in the New World setting up a "grammar school" in every jurisdiction of fifty householders. The stated intention of the law was to teach writing and reading so as to combat ignorance of the Scriptures, which ignorance was the "one chief project of that ould deluder, Satan." Another intention, however, obtrudes later in the act, when the purpose of schools and masters is also said to be "to instruct youth so farr as they shall be fitted for the university." There would be no University, so called, for over two hundred years, but in 1647 a coherent set of values, informing a basic system of schools, could project a limitless educational ideal along a continuum available to the mind, if not yet to the eye.

From the earliest days of the colonies and long past the Constitution's legal separation of Church and State, schools were the local expressions of a unified political and religious culture. They promoted the religious beliefs, which were also political beliefs, that were tightly tied to localities. The pre-Revolutionary schools and colleges lost their character only gradually as containers of unified religious and political systems of value, but they had by the turning of the eighteenth century already bequeathed to the new republic a tradition that was to be one of America's most enduring: the tradition of local control over schools and the educational principles that animate a town or region. That tradition of local control persists to this day, although by the nineteenth century schools were no longer the vehicles for religious values but had become instruments of federal policy, expanding with the land as it opened up—now secular, aimed at utilitarian goals and the promotion of economic expansion.

This simplified sketch means that there was, during the early days of the Republic, in the terms school and education, a competing set of local and national aspirations. One can read these competing but fused aspirations into the fabulous sentence that opens article three of the Northwest Ordinance, passed on July 17, 1787: "Religion, morality, and knowledge, being necessary to good government and the happiness of mankind, schools and the means of education shall forever by encouraged." This prophetic fusion of individual entities and general means, willing unity while assuming diversity, is a version of the competing ideals that shaped our nation and its life. One sees this competition and fusion again clearly when President Madison, in his second message to Congress on December 5, 1810, finds it necessary to argue for a national university by denying its national character. "Such an institu-

155

tion," says Madison, "though local in legal character, would be universal in its beneficial effects."*
Madison emphasizes the particular, not the general,
character of a national, not a local, entity.

In Madison's argument for a local national school
with universal benefits, he combines, by an act of
rhetorical will, inherently different concepts for the
public good and the local autonomy. In this willed
fusion of competing theories we recognize the outlines of the tension between education and school
first hinted at in the third article of the Northwest
Ordinance, and expressed at its largest in the tension
between potent assertions of principle regarding
all of humankind and a radical belief in the unique
essence and prerogatives of the individual. The management of this larger tension is our history: in
terms of our topic, historically, it means that education is a civilizing process for the general good and
school is the local expression of specific, utilitarian
needs, and that these concepts ought to go together
even if they do not go easily.

Our present-day confusion about our schools and
the role of an education does not occur, I believe,
because we have resolved this tension. It occurs
because we have lost the tension. We have lost it
by allowing the utilitarian view of school to displace
the larger educational perspective. In losing it we
have lost touch with our past, with the fructifying

* Cited in the excellent study by George N. Rainsford,
Congress and Higher Education in the Nineteenth Century
(Knoxville: University of Tennessee Press, 1972), p. 20.

156

energy that the older tension, fully embraced, could inspire. We have lost the will to keep a civil ideal and a utilitarian entity together in balance, and thus we have insured the success of neither one nor the other. Schools now do not educate, we are told, nor do they prepare people to be employed; they neither promote a civic regard for the values of the larger society nor do they adequately prepare individuals to be working or employable adults. Without a larger educational ethic the school is treated only as a machine, churning out an unemployable product, and is inevitably perceived as another failure of an industrialized society.

Yet, where it is seen as having failed most, in the inner city, the public school can afford least to fail. The American educational dream, after all, is no secret. That educational dream is most bitterly recalled precisely where America's most recent immigrants and longest oppressed are gathered. There the basic American educational ideal must be most alive, and it is not. This country, however, cannot turn its back on its poor and jobless; it cannot think that its ideals of equal opportunity and social mobility are too difficult to implant or cultivate among the urban or migrant poor. America cannot either by denial or deferral allow itself to transform the public schools into warehouses for the angry or staging areas for anarchy. There must be a commitment to keep the tension between values and utility alive, so that hope will inspire information and the promise of access will elevate utility. American history and its promises, formed through our schools and means of education, cannot be denied to any of our people lest our society rot with the failure to bring its professions of hope for all into conjunction with its daily reality.

Let us look back at some documents of our public life for a moment, not to study the nostalgias but to regather the complexity of willed beliefs and complementary tensions which formed our practical vision of civility. My intention is briefly to explore the meaning of the language of the third article of the Northwest Ordinance, that good government and the happiness of mankind must be encouraged not only through the promotion of schools, but by the means of education as well. I choose three texts, from three different periods of our history, by three very different authors.

TEXT I. 1848. Horace Mann, Secretary of the Massachusetts State Board of Education, in his twelfth annual report. In the land of Emerson, the lyceum movement and Brook Farm, Mann is imbued with a utopian idealism; he believes that in a society riven by economic and social inequality, a leaden reality can be transmuted to a golden egalitarianism by the touchstone of universal public education. He notes the wide disparity in his time and place of the rich and poor; he asks if "competence can displace pauperism," and he answers that only "universal education can counterwork this tendency to the domination of capital and the servility of labor."

Education then, beyond all other devices of human origin, is a great equalizer of the conditions of men,—the balance wheel of the social machinery. I do not here mean that it so elevates the moral nature as to make men disdain and abhor the oppression of their fellow men. This idea pertains to another of its attributes. But I mean that it gives each man the independence and the means by which he can resist the selfishness of other men. It does better than to disarm the poor of their hostility toward the rich: it prevents being poor.

This practical Transcendentalism envisions a world ultimately made secure and moral by education because it initially envisions schooling as minting the ore of the mind.

That political economy, therefore, which busies itself about capital and labor, supply and demand, interests and rents, favorable and unfavorable balances of trade, but leaves out of account the elements of a wide-spread mental development, is naught but stupendous folly.

Public schooling is education for civility because it prepares one for fruitful and productive work, and work in the world is the way to dignity and equality. As shrewd as it is idealistic, Mann's vision is at the core, practical and civic, of the American educational dream.

159

TEXT II. January 28, 1915. President Wilson vetoing, as Presidents Cleveland and Taft had before him, an act of Congress requiring literacy tests for new immigrants. (The act would pass over his veto in 1917). Literacy is access in American society, thus through our history those negative tributes to its power: the slave codes which forbade teaching black people to read and write; the Congress' desire to prohibit access to America by millions of foreigners looking for work and a better life by requiring literacy where it could not always exist. Wilson believes this act is "a radical departure" from the principles and tradition of the nation.

> It seeks to all but close entirely the gates of asylum which have always been open to those who could find nowhere else the right and opportunity of constitutional agitation for what they conceived to be the natural and inalienable rights of men; and it excludes those to whom the opportunities of elementary education have been denied, without regard to their character, their purposes, or their natural capacity.

Access to America denied because literacy is absent means

> Those who come seeking opportunity are not to be admitted unless they have already had one of the chief of the opportunities they seek, the opportunity of education.

160

For Wilson, education is one of the prime opportunities promised by America, not a prerequisite for opportunity in America. As for Mann, so for Wilson but on a broader scale, educational opportunity defines America and is the means by which to make oneself an American.

TEXT III. 1940. Associate Justice Felix Frankfurter in the case of *Minersville School District* v. *Gobitis*. The Gobitis children had been expelled from public school in Pennsylvania for refusing, according to their principles as Jehovah's Witnesses, to salute the flag. Their father sued to enjoin the Minersville school board from requiring a salute to the flag as part of school, and the district and circuit courts found for Mr. Gobitis. Frankfurter reversed the lower courts. In his opinion in 1940, however, one finds a moving affirmation of what we first noticed: the power of the school context and the educational process to unify a polity and to preserve the individual—that quintessentially American act of the will that fuses public values and private integrity in a circuit of mutual responsibility, with education at the center.

First, Frankfurter asserts, through the symbol of the flag, the larger values of society:

> The ultimate foundation of a free society is the binding ties of cohesive sentiment. Such a sentiment is fostered by all those agencies of the mind and spirit which may serve to gather up

161

the traditions of a people, transmit them from generation to generation, and thereby create that continuity of a treasured common life which constitutes a civilization.

One may infer that not only the flag, but also the schoolroom—when more than simply schooling occurs—also contains and continues the treasured common life that constitutes a civilization. Frankfurter then turns from the society's binding values to the rights of individuals, here figured as states or school boards and, by implication, private persons:

The precise issue, then, for us to decide is whether the legislatures of the various states and the authorities in a thousand counties and school districts of this country are barred from determining the appropriateness of various means to evoke that unifying sentiment without which there can ultimately be no liberties, civil or religious.

He returns at the end of his meditation, in a long paragraph, to a comprehensive view of the ordered society and of the individual's liberty, a view and paragraph where conceptually and structurally the educational process is placed between society and the individual, at the center:

The preciousness of the family relation, the authority and independence which give dignity to parenthood, indeed the enjoyment of all freedom, presupposes the kind of ordered society

162

which is summarized by our flag. A society which is dedicated to the preservation of these ultimate values of civilization may in self-protection utilize the educational process for inculcating those almost unconscious feelings which bind men together in a comprehending loyalty, whatever may be their lesser differences and difficulties. That is to say, the process may be utilized as long as men's right to believe as they please, to win others to their way of belief, and their right to assemble in their chosen places of worship for the devotional ceremonies of their faith, are all fully respected.

This willed harmony between the larger public good and the sacred individual liberties, a harmony embodied in and nourished by the educational process, is the challenge—difficult, delicate, requiring constant effort—of the American educational dream that must be realized in the schools. In their differing ways, Mann, Wilson and Frankfurter all believe education is an intangible but definable assertion of moral courage that turns schooling into civilization. In that moral act is the willed assertion that says a polity must be made through a process that is not merely political; in it is a belief in the continuous transmission of values without the imposition of a specific religious belief. In it is a voluntary assent to the binding proposition that individual freedoms must be directed to a general order which alone will preserve those freedoms. Education has been the training for this multiple act of will and belief and consent and, in terms of our history, education has been one of our chief means to preserve the willed act that is America.

When confronted with competing and confusing pressures, we Americans always return to those original assertions of principle that first managed our tensions and taught us to measure our several freedoms and greater order. It is time to recollect again the parts of that vision, for when we ask what shall be done about our public schools, we are asking what shall be done about the future of our country. And before the numbering of programs and policies, entitlements and amendments and appropriations begins; before we slay forests to promote more of a paper thicket of memos, mandates and moans, let us reassert the recollected vision: that education is first the responsibility of the family, and of the householders with or without children in the schools, and of the teachers, and of the local boards, all working together, no one assuming that the others can bear such a responsibility alone.

Before we allow political leaders, wherever they are, to fall silent and turn from the intractable problems, let us remind them that some responsible voice must urge values from the center on behalf of the people, values that assert the primary importance of quality in instruction and equality of opportunity in our schools, for without that voice the schools will have no tendency, no larger, enlarging civic mission.

Before more policies and programmatic initiatives sweep over us, let us remember that the partnership of parents and neighbors, civic leaders and politicians, must first agree that the schools are the most important single asset the community holds in common. Let us assert that the duty of that partnership at home is to decide that the first priority for public money, through taxes and bonds, is the school system. And let us then insist that the partners insist that schools have a role and obligation in the treasured common life beyond mere schooling.

And when we have reassembled a vision of the purpose of school and of the means of education, then we can pass to the rebuilding of what is both a system and a process of civility. To lament only, or to paper over the cracks in schools with scarce dollars with no idea of the point of it all; to bring up our children to live alone, not with others, would be stupendous folly. That would be to accept the lie that we are a people without purpose and that excellence and equality cannot still be the unlimited aspiration of all our people. We must study therefore, not the bygone simplicities or the new limits, but the old complexities that made our dream a reality. Before programs and policies, we must reconnect with and revive the grand vision of our first principles and practicalities.

Power, Politics and
a Sense of History

One of our most sensible commentators on education and society recently published a brief piece which was deeply disturbing for what it said, yet again, about America's confusion about ideas and power and the power of ideas in our national life. Briefly, this commentator, dismayed because Professor James Coleman had authored a report holding "that private high schools seemed to provide a better education than public ones," went to considerable lengths to chide social scientists for having or wishing to have an impact on the course and conduct of national life. Thinking about society is splendid, it seemed to say, as long as the thinkers remain uninvolved in public policy and its creation. "Sociology gains in prestige and value when it keeps its distance from the political battles of the day."*

* *The New York Times*, May 11, 1981, The Editorial Notebook.

166

Presumably, politicians, who fight the battles of the day, fight them better when they do not have the benefit of thinking. Why, thoughtful people have chosen to join the gang on the crowded anti-social science bandwagon is a question I cannot answer. Most disturbing to me is the idea that "If those who wield political power are to make use of sociological studies—and they should—the research should be neutral both in fact and appearance." I believe our commentator wants research that is nonpartisan, as do I. If he wants, however, social science research that is encouraged to believe itself free of values and disconnected from the world it studies, then he wants soulless, "academic" theorizing that will be of no use to anyone.

To wish a world where ideas are "value free," freeze-dried commodities, and political power is necessarily unconnected with reflection or analysis about society, is to wish for more of what we have at a time when we need much less of it. Our problem as a society is that we have fostered disconnectedness; we have created a false separateness between social research and policy making, thinking and politics, ideas and power. At some point we became unmoored from that fundamental Western concept of a society where the leader and the system he energizes were meant to blend thought and action, ideas with force and forceful ethical behavior. Read Plato's *Statesman*, where the leader fosters education and education furthers the weaving of the web of the state, meshing as in a tapestry the various types of citizens; read Cicero's

Republic, where the state is a harmonious orchestra, blending like musical tones the various classes, a concord aided by an idea of justice; read these, and whatever you think of them, you will not find a vision of a state where ideas and power can be distinct, where the power of ideas could ever be unconnected to a forceful public good.

For those whose education has been for the purpose of directing ideas to a life of leadership and service to others, whose education has been to see and feel and think about the connectedness among things and how that connectedness must be fostered so that civilization is sustained, my theme is power and a sense of history in our public life. What concerns me most is the way we have disconnected ideas from power in America and created for ourselves thoughtful citizens who disdain politics and politicians, when more than ever we need to value politics and what politicians do; when more than ever we need to recognize that the calling to public life is one of the highest callings a society can make. We need to recognize that if we do not summon and send forth from ourselves a few of the highest quality to lead, the many cannot hold together in civility and dignity.

If a society assumes its politicians are venal, stupid or self-serving, it will attract to its public life as an ongoing self-fulfilling prophecy the greedy, the knavish and the dim. If, as I will argue later, a culture like ours has wrongly persuaded itself that power is really

168

mere force, and the use of power in its public or private life simply the exercise of force, then that culture will attract to leadership those who misunderstand power and who therefore cannot possibly use it correctly or well. How power is conceived in a society has the most to do with determining who is attracted to positions of power. A healthy society must never wish to have as its public servants people who only hunger to be in public life, who, thinking power is a natural force, believe they will become immortal if they can tap into its sheer, natural flow. The best way to avoid such people is to avoid such an idea of power.

Far better to think historically, to remember the lessons of the past. Thus, far better to conceive of power as consisting in part of the knowledge of when not to use all the power you have. Far better to be one who knows that if you reserve the power not to use all your power, you will lead others far more successfully and well, for to restrain power is in effect to share it. To share power is to give power to those who do not have it. Whoever knows how to restrain and effectively release power finds, if he is skillful and good, that power flows back to him. Power flows back to such a leader because from the sharing of power comes stability in a society, and stability is finally what humankind aches for, a stability that is just and equitable and humane. On the other hand, those who think of power as simple force to be unleashed, force of personality, force of followers, force of might, force with no historical roots and no sense of consequence, invariably find that they exhaust their power, or are exhausted by it; they find that they only call forth their opposites and that then society inevitably swings, sickeningly, back and forth among those thoughtless enough to consume power because they will not share, and thus replenish, it. Under such leaders, the body politic suffers seizures but it never achieves stability. No one wins.

This layman's view of how power in a democracy ought to be construed depends for its efficacy upon those who are attracted to public life; it requires those who are impelled by talent for connectedness rather than by ambition for aggrandized private pleasure; its efficacy depends upon politicians who view the act of governing not as the exercise of sheer pressure, but as the assertion of compelling principle. I believe that we have a number of such people serving at the local and national level, and that we do not appreciate them as we should. I also believe we ought to be concerned by the spectacle of so many experienced and able elected officials, at all levels, retiring from public service because they will no longer put up with the casual unappreciation by the very people who elected them or with the gnawing of special-interest groups or with the constant high whine emitted by the herds of lobbyists. Finally, we must recognize that we have been so disdainful of or inattentive to our political system that it is increasingly difficult to find candidates who assume the need for any measure of professionalism as a prerequisite for public service.

By professionalism in politics I mean that one should serve an apprenticeship in how to serve, that women and men be encouraged and trained in how to be responsive in a democracy as well as responsible for democratic values. Increasingly we elect, on the basis of powerful advertising campaigns, people who do not know how to do anything for anybody, whether it is having a street light installed or protecting a citizen against loss of liberty. Increasingly we elect people who are governed by their staffs, whom no one elected. By professionalism, I mean we must find people who know how and when to subordinate personal obsession to the wishes or will of those they represent, wishes or will those politicians comprehend by returning to where they came from to talk to the people, not by counting editorials or by reading polls. People with professionalism believe politics is an ancient art, not a necessary trial in the world for secular saints or a new game to be played after the rigors of making money are over. Professionalism in public life would never assume that you educate the citizenry to its needs by asserting over and over again that government is best done by dismantling the structures and purposes of government.

While it pleases some to repeat that politics is the art of the possible, I prefer to think that politicians must have the capacity for the impossible—for knowing in which direction their moral compass points and for being supple enough to persuade others of the moral rightness of the course they have set. They must be those who have a clear sense of how complex

171

life is and be willing to make choices they can then convince other thinking people are the correct decisions. We are afflicted now, and have been for some time, with solo operators for whom nothing is complex, because nothing is connected to anything else; who believe the function of government is to impose moralistic schemes rather than to forge complex consensuses, and who treat government as an impediment to mandating purity rather than as a means of connecting, and negotiating among, legitimate needs and achieving a practical, equitable balance. I am disheartened that for at least a decade we have been told by our shepherds that government or the other shepherds are the "enemy." Government is not the enemy, and neither are the people who elect governments. If we elect those who play on the forces that divide us, who play to our fears, we court a tragedy we may not be able to contain. And if we continue to elect those who denigrate what they pursue, who insist they are outsiders as they claw their way to the inside, we ought to ask if it is in our common interest to buy any more snake oil.

Where did it all start in our culture, this worship of power as force, this contempt for restraining or complex connections, and the consequent devaluation of political life? I am not really sure but I choose to speculate it began in the middle of the last century, as America was collapsing into and struggling out of the ruins of the Civil War. I think it began with those

172

who were best positioned to bypass the Founders and to summon up the original strength of Puritan America and to hurl that strength, naked, squalling as if newborn, into the gathering darkness. I believe it began with prophets of the secular religion that was the new America, like Emerson. In 1860, Emerson published his essay "Power" in *The Conduct of Life.*

In the dark pages of that powerful meditation on power, on the eve of the War, Emerson amply reflects a view of politics and politicians that is disdainful of the hurly-burly, the compromising, and the dirtiness of it all. But Emerson makes it clear that he does not share those fastidious views. Those views, he says, are only held by the "timid man"; by the "churchmen and men of refinement," implicitly effete and bookish. Emerson was not for them. He was for the man who is strong, healthy, unfettered, the man who knows that nothing is got for nothing and who will stop at nothing to put himself in touch with events and their force. He is willing to say, because he believes it, that "Society is a troop of thinkers, and the best heads among them take the best places," but the metaphor of the mounted squadron, with the best jostling to the fore, means that this is a special kind of thinker. He is, as the immediately preceding sentence says, one who knows "There is always room for a man of force, and he makes room for many." The "thinkers" Emerson really admires are those with "coarse energy,—the 'bruisers,' who have run the gauntlet of caucus and tavern through the county or the state,—" the politicians who despite their vices have "the good-nature of strength and courage." And what do the political bruisers know? They know what Emerson knows:

> the key to all ages is—Imbecility; imbecility in the vast majority of men at all times, and even in heroes in all but certain eminent moments; victims of gravity, custom, and fear. This gives force to the strong,—that the multitude have no habit of self-reliance or original action.

With extraordinary literary skills at a crucial moment in our nation's life, it is Emerson who freed our politics and our politicians from any sense of restraint by extolling self-generated, unaffiliated power as the best foot to place in the small of the back of the man in front of you, and who promoted shoving as the highest calling abolitionist, moral New England could conceive.

Emerson was a potent figure in his time, and his influence in our culture is powerful to this day. You do not have to read the prophet to realize his ideas are all around us. Strangely enough, he lives in the popular imagination as the Lover of Nature, a sweet, sentimental, Yankee Kahlil Gibran. In fact, Emerson is as sweet as barbed wire, and his sentimentality as accommodating as a brick. There might have been no lasting harm in all this, no lasting harm in his hymns to the strong and to a strength deriving from a frenzied harmony with the higher laws of Nature; no great harm, though enough, from his wishing for a politics where energy, will and ferocious concentration were the royal roads to success; no real danger from his worship of "self-reliance and original action," except that, like all implacable saviors, Emerson knew where his people were most insecure and where he could best make his balm as indispensable as blood. His everlasting harm comes because he knew Americans would forever feel themselves colonists and thus forever feel themselves derived, or secondhand. And so his greatest contribution to our culture, and greatest disservice, lies in the assurances with which in subtle and obvious ways he justified jettisoning history.

Emerson found in our independent character xenophobia, and he made it into a gospel. He managed to persuade generations that custom was a crutch, not a means of continuity; he assured everyman that he was his own pure source, and that every native strain in his character was a link with Higher Nature. He wished to sever America from Europe, and American culture and scholarship and politics from whatever humankind had fashioned before. And he thought he had done something good.

The result is that he infected American culture with a scorn of the past. The result is he encouraged America to shake loose from any constraint on our strength and then to call the resulting power miraculous because it had no moorings. Thus, to Emerson I believe we owe our worship of a politics which wishes for originality in all things: for a society in its origins pure, for solutions that are wondrously complete, for politicians whose sheer unthinking vigor will cleanse us forever. To Emerson we owe that spirit of Puritan America that has survived to today, the smug, abstract moralism that is distrustful of any accommodation, that is always certain of its righteousness because it is merely self-regarding, that is scornful of any flexibility of spirit because it has never looked over its shoulder. Emerson and those who followed him licensed that unstable strain in us that would have us begin all over again every morning, every morning to discover evil again in order every morning to focus the will in order to shove our way to noontime; that naive energy that legitimizes those gusts of moralistic frenzy masquerading as high principle that periodically seize us by the throat and that, while always comfortable with nostalgia, are never truly attentive to history. Emerson licensed our violent swings from extreme to extreme by insisting that whatever willful impulse sat in the throne of the heart holds legitimate sway. In another creed, his self-reliance would be the sin of pride.

Rootless save for immersion in the rich soil of the endlessly admiring self, glowing with animal energy, completely devoid of any sense of our common past, a new technocrat of force, Emerson's figure of power formed more than the nineteenth and much of the twentieth centuries' view of the politician. It formed what became an acceptable public personality, and that view of power and its uses is still with us; and it still calls forth reactions to itself as extreme as it is.

That is why I lay at Emerson's cottage door the encouragement to instability that is one of America's real afflictions.

Emerson's views are those of a brazen adolescent and we ought to be rid of them. The maturing of America will occur when we have absorbed, not rejected, our past, our past as various peoples from diverse cultures, not simply as entrepreneurs of the soul. We will mature fully when we require a sense of history in those who lead us, and reject those originals who believe, in whatever walk of life, that each of us is created afresh solely for the purpose of baying at every new, pure moon. The maturing of our politics, which is to say the fashioning of our national life as a work of art, will come when stability of society, not originality of action, is our goal.

To assume that civility—and not success in forcing new purities—is the proper end of politics is to begin to rid this country of the extraordinary savagery of spirit that is now abroad: the resentment at the advancement of others, the bitterness that begrudges everyone else everything, the increasing and deeply dangerous polarization of the races, the pustular eruptions of sexism, racism and of anti-Semitism whose stench now fills the air. These are all signs that some now feel licensed to shove again the less numerous, the weaker, the new, the exotic, the foreign. I smell that spirit in the air and read it in the papers, I see it in the mail I get, I read it spray-painted on walls, I hear it in the jokes people tell, and it is imperative that all of us condemn and exorcise that spirit. We must civilly, but absolutely clearly reject a spirit that instinctively turns to boycott, instead of tough, reasoned debate, to express its disagreement. We must publicly reject the movement that once again cries to ban books in libraries. We must insist on law, not on rule by decree; we must insist that the principles of the Constitution be applied through the courts and resist the desire that the Constitution be endlessly amended. We must never lose sight of the need for a balanced, pluralistic society, where ideas compete and principles are adjudged by legislative processes and judicial forums. If the day is won by the neo-Puritans through those means, so be it. But those who simply, arrogantly assert that their morality is in the majority should not expect others who simply do not believe it to stand mute. A civil society can be shattered by the kind of coercion that now seeks to become commonplace.

These tensions and many others are the stuff of our local and national public life, and must be managed by our politicians and by the rest of us. We should honor those who are willing to confront them and we must insist that they and we do not acquiesce to their divisive force. We must encourage a regard for those who manage our public needs and desires and if we do not find that regard justified, then we must find and encourage those in whom we can believe and who are worthy of our trust. We must insist that the goal of our politics is not punishment of some group or tendency, but healing, a healing of the wounds that the world will always inflict on us all; we must remember and insist that our leaders know that exclusion was never the purpose of our country's dream. We must remember America was not founded to create exiles.

America's founders intended that we manage, by an act of the will, competing as well as complementary freedoms, in the interests of forging a civil state and a free, generous people. That is not impossibly high idealism and we cannot let our public life fall to disconnected fragments by scorning its call, or by ignoring its imperatives. High idealism is America's most practical and durable product, our best native handicraft. Those who founded this Republic knew that and it is the obligation of our political leaders and of the rest of us who elect them to remember it too. It is our obligation to remember that the promise of our history lives in each of us as a sacred trust. What a grand and precious gift, that legacy of competing freedoms all urging us to liberality of spirit and a decent public order.

Coda: The Codification of Us All

I propose here to focus on what I take to be some of the deep, shaping forces moving through our universities and to pause over one of those forces for a while. Let us agree that great American universities, public and private, are nineteenth-century creations: unique intersections of a Germanic, research hierarchy and a broad set of democratic values, of which access, equity and the striving for quality were and are the most prominent. These amalgams of a European structure and a set of native values are uniquely American, and these institutions managed the tension between an exclusive form and an inclusive philosophy, between a structure satisfactory for the encouragement of quality and a perspective necessary to the fostering of opportunity, until the Second World War. Perhaps longer. More than a hundred years, from just after mid-century to just after mid-century. And if you will assume that paradigm, which may be a good deal to ask, then let me assert that, in the last twenty years, the old solution represented by the American university to the problem of propagating democratic values by way of a generally oligarchic structure has begun to change. It is changing because of three movements: a tendency toward forms of decentralization, as the diffusion of power has been followed by the diffusion of money; the increasingly corporate nature of universities, as one of the great inventions of twentieth-century America, the private industrial corporation, has begun to displace, as a formal structure and as a style of management, the older ecclesiastical and academic structures and styles in which universities grew up; and finally, an impulse that I can only call the codification of the academy. This is the once gradual, now visible and ever accelerating effort to encapsulate all values in codes. It is the effort to capture what at its best was a consensus—that universities were collegial institutions designed to foster within, and promote without, access, equity and intellectual excellence—and to put that consensus into a code.

It is this last movement across universities that most interests me. A code is a reduction of an ideal and will always fall short by virtue of the simple fact that language is not capable of incorporating reality, much less an ideal. A code no more describes or improves upon a consensus than a train schedule describes or improves upon a journey. A consensus of shared values must always be prepared for new in- to connote a feeling with, or a mutuality of, shared values does not by that act of documentation insure the persistence of consensus. Indeed, if consensus is taken in its root meaning as derived from Latin to connote a feeling with, or a mutuality of, shared sentiment, then the act of documentation may be the best way to note the demise of consensus.

Within the University, within the country, for the University is only a reflection of the country, there would be any number of ways of demonstrating the increasing triumph of the impulse to codify. One could, as I once did in some remarks about federal regulation and basic research, argue that the cod- ification of the academy stems largely from the fed- eral government and that finally what will be lost will be the essential collegiality of these institutions, the shared sense of trust in others' shared sense of value, as university administrations increasingly be- come the custodians of codes they do not necessarily understand, and faculty members become the cus- todians of values, the older values of access, equity and intellectual excellence, that the codes wish to promote but cannot encompass. The sundering of the academy, the splitting apart of administrators and faculties, is going on for far deeper and longer- range reasons than simply the fairly recent demo- graphic and inflationary pressures with which all academic communities live. This view of the cod- ification of the academy, that sees external regulation shredding not stitching internal collegiality, is a view I have expressed and hold.

I also think, however, there is another side to the question. That side emerges when one considers that the values universities say they cherish and foster and promote have not always been fostered, cherished and promoted within them; when one considers that the society has been urged by universities to encourage access and attend to equity and excellence, but that when the broadest forms of these values, documented in codes and reduced but still energized by regulation, come back to the academy in a shape the academy does not recognize, only then do problems arise. But the return of the very values that, at its best, the American university said it wished to see adopted should not surprise the academic community, unless that community is surprised by the success of its teaching and best behavior. All I am saying is that the increasing codification of the academy, which will lose us something very valuable, is occurring because something equally valuable—a belief that merit and access are not incompatible, that excellence and equal opportunity can go hand in hand—is now a widespread national conviction. And even the academy, that said the new values were valid, must act according to its professed beliefs.

I do not presume to know whether in the collision of values, or worlds of shared assumptions, about what constitutes civilized life, more is inevitably lost than is possibly gained. All I hope is that the codification to which I refer is a transitory phenomenon; that, without taking a position I have not yet earned on whether law is the reforming engine of society or the mirror reflecting society's state, we do not depend upon law for all our ideals; that we do not believe codes are more than ghostly sketches of consensus; that we do not as citizens go easily to the proposition that until everything is written down it does not exist; and that we resist the desire to wish for a past world where absolutes looked neater, easier, more agreeable precisely because they were known only to a few, even if preached to the many.

I think this University is carefully engaging in the process of dismantling a set of shared assumptions by the very act of fashioning public expressions of what were once only private privileges. This process is one that calls neither for strident applause nor for plangent lament but rather for a reasoned recognition that Nothing comes for Nothing. In such matters we do best when we remember institutions change so they may endure, endure with a sense of their purpose and dignity, which sense is what differentiates endurance from mere survival. What I see happening in the university, a wiser soul might be able to see happening in the whole country. Such an assertion would not startle me, but I leave that kind of vision to my betters.

A. Bartlett Giamatti

A. Bartlett Giamatti was born in Boston in 1938, grew up in South Hadley, Massachusetts and Rome, and attended Yale College and the Yale Graduate School. He taught Italian and Comparative Literature at Princeton University and joined the Yale faculty in 1966. Mr. Giamatti was the John Hay Whitney Professor of English and Comparative Literature at Yale when he was named nineteenth president of the University in 1977. He is married to Toni Smith Giamatti, a teacher, and they have three children.